THE
DIALOGUE
THESAURUS

*A Fiction Writer's Sourcebook of
Dialogue Tags and Phrases*

DAHLIA EVANS

For Mum

Contents

Introduction   *1*

PART 1 – Dialogue and Action Tags

Dialogue and Action Tags in Alphabetical Order   *3*
Emotion: Anger   *7*
Emotion: Fear   *7*
Emotion: Happiness   *8*
Emotion: Love   *9*
Emotion: Sadness   *9*
Emotion: Surprise   *10*
Dynamics: Loud   *10*
Dynamics: Soft   *11*

PART 2 – Dialogue Adverbs

Adverbs in Alphabetical Order   *12*
Emotion: Anger   *27*
Emotion: Fear   *28*
Emotion: Happiness   *29*
Emotion: Love   *30*
Emotion: Sadness   *32*
Emotion: Surprise   *33*
Emotion: Unfeeling   *34*
Dynamics: Loud   *34*
Dynamics: Soft   *35*
Sound: Tone   *36*
Physical State: Hungry / Thirsty   *36*
Physical State: Sick   *37*
Physical State: Tired   *37*
Manner: Bored   *38*
Manner: Confused   *39*
Manner: Critical   *40*
Manner: Deceptive   *40*

Manner: Disgusted   *41*
Manner: Embarrassed   *42*
Manner: Jealous   *42*
Manner: Pandering   *43*
Manner: Polite   *44*
Manner: Proud / Austere   *45*
Manner: Rude   *46*
Manner: Serious / Rational   *46*
Manner: Stubborn   *48*
Manner: Truthful   *48*
Manner: Vague   *49*

PART 3 – Feelings, Emotions, and Internal Dialogue

Feelings and Emotions in Alphabetical Order   *50*
Emotion: Anger   *72*
Emotion: Fear   *73*
Emotion: Happiness   *74*
Emotion: Love   *75*
Emotion: Sadness   *76*
Emotion: Surprise   *78*
Emotion: Unfeeling   *78*
Physical State: Hungry / Thirsty   *79*
Physical State: Sick   *80*
Physical State: Tired   *80*
Manner: Bored   *81*
Manner: Confused   *82*
Manner: Critical   *83*
Manner: Deceptive   *83*
Manner: Disgusted   *84*
Manner: Embarrassed   *85*
Manner: Jealous   *85*
Manner: Pandering   *86*
Manner: Polite   *87*
Manner: Proud / Austere   *88*
Manner: Rude   *89*
Manner: Serious / Rational   *89*
Manner: Stubborn   *90*
Manner: Truthful   *91*
Modifying Words   *91*
Internal Dialogue and Thought Tags   *92*

PART 4 – Body Language and Movement

Arms   *93*
Arms: Fingers   *95*
Arms: Hands / Palms   *96*
Body   *99*
Body: Heart   *102*
Body: Shoulders   *104*
Body: Skin / Flesh   *106*
Body: Spine   *107*
Body: Stomach   *109*
Body: Throat   *110*
Eyes   *114*
Face   *119*
Face: Cheeks   *123*
Face: Eyebrows / Brows   *125*
Hair   *127*
Head / Forehead   *130*
Mouth   *133*
Mouth: Breathed   *135*
Mouth: Laughed   *138*
Mouth: Lips   *140*
Mouth: Smile   *144*
Mouth: Teeth   *149*
Mouth: Voice   *152*
Nose   *157*

Also by Dahlia Evans

Introduction

The idea for this book came about while I was analyzing the structure of various novels. As part of the exercise, I decided to see if I could somehow catalogue the words and phrases that surround fictional dialogue. It wasn't long before I discovered a number of patterns. This was a eureka moment in my writing career.

I then asked myself a question: *"Should I keep this information to myself? Or instead, share it with the writing community."* Knowing how much this information would help budding and professional writers alike, I decided to share it by writing this book.

For me, this thesaurus is a book I didn't realize I needed. But now that I have it sitting in front of me, I can't imagine writing fictional dialogue without it. I no longer need to rack my brain to come up with fitting dialogue tags and phrases. Now, I just open this book and away I go! I hope you will have a similar experience.

How This Book Is Organized

The book is broken up into four parts. They are: *dialogue and action tags*; *dialogue adverbs*; *feelings, emotions, and internal dialogue*; and *body language and movement*.

In the first three parts all words are sorted in alphabetical order, as well as grouped by category. These categories include: *emotion*; *dynamics*; *sound*; *physical state*; and *manner*.

Part Three also includes the following two categories: *modifying words*; and *internal dialogue and thought tags*.

Entries for parts *One* to *Three* are separated by a semicolon.

Part Four is structured slightly differently. Entries are sorted by physical feature; with each entry separated by a line break.

Example sentences *('USAGE EXAMPLES')* are used at the end of each category to give the reader an idea of how to use an entry in a dialogue sequence. Each entry is italicized.

How to Use This Book

1) I'm sick of using 'he said' and 'she said' so often. I want some variety!

In this case, go to *PART 1 – Dialogue and Action Tags* and select a tag; either by alphabet, or by category. If you know what type of emotion you wish to express – and that emotion is included – select a word that fits your dialogue.

2) *I want to use an adverb to add a little spice.*

Adverbs, if used sparingly, can add a spark to your dialogue writing. No matter what any critic says, adverbs will always have a place in fiction. Just remember: quality over quantity. *PART 2 – Dialogue Adverbs* includes pretty much every usable adverb that can be combined with *'said'* (or other dialogue tags).

3) *My dialogue is ambiguous, so I want to explain what the character is feeling.*

In this case, go to *PART 3 – Feelings, Emotions, and Internal Dialogue.* Here you will find every major feeling and emotion word out there. Using the *Modifying Words* category will give you some ideas when structuring your sentences.

If you want to write internal dialogue then go to the category: *Internal Dialogue and Thought Tags* for a great selection of tags.

4) *I want to show the character's actions to help the reader visualize the scene.*

PART 4 – Body Language and Movement gives you everything you need to describe a character's body language and movement. These phrases will bring your dialogue to life!

While you can use these phrases as they are, it is my hope that you will also use them as inspiration to come up with your own variations. Combine, rearrange, and alter 'til your heart's content.

Finally, I want to thank you for your investment. I hope this thesaurus aids you in all your future writing projects.

Warm Wishes,
Dahlia Evans

1
Dialogue and Action Tags

Dialogue tags and *action tags* are used to indicate to the reader which character is speaking. Tags are also used to convey the tone or quality of the character's voice.

Dialogue and Action Tags in Alphabetical Order

A
abjured; accused; acknowledged; added; addressed; admitted; admonished; advertised; advised; advocated; affirmed; agonized; agreed; alleged; alluded; announced; answered; apologized; appealed; approved; argued; arranged; articulated; asked; assented; asserted; asseverated; assumed; assured; attested; averred; avowed.

B
babbled; baited; bantered; bargained; barked; bawled; beamed; beckoned; began; begged; belittled; bellowed; berated; beseeched; bit out; blasted; blazed; bleated; blew up; blubbered; blurted; blurted out; blustered; boasted; boomed; bossed; bragged; breathed; broached; broadcast; broke in; bubbled; bugged; bullied; burst out.

C
cackled; cajoled; calculated; called; called out; caroled; carped; cautioned; censured; challenged; chanted; charged; chatted; chattered; cheered; chided; chimed in; chipped in; choked; choked out; chortled; chorused; chuckled; circulated; cited; claimed; clucked; coaxed; comforted; commanded; commented; communicated; complained; completed; complimented; conceded; concluded; concurred; condemned; condescended; conferred; confessed; confided; confirmed; confuted; congratulated; consented; consoled; contended; contested; continued; contradicted; contributed; convinced; cooed; corrected; coughed;

counseled; countered; crabbed; cracked; craved; cried; cried out; criticized; croaked; crooned; cross-examined; crowed; cursed.

D
dared; debated; decided; declared; decreed; defended; defied (her/him); delivered; demanded; demurred; denied; denoted; denounced; described; dictated; dinned; directed; disagreed; disclaimed; disclosed; disposed; disrupted; disseminated; divulged; doted; doubted; drawled; droned.

E
echoed; ejaculated; elaborated; emitted; empathized; emphasized; encouraged; ended; enjoined; entreated; enumerated; enunciated; equivocated; estimated; exacted; exaggerated; exclaimed; exhorted; expatiated; explained; exploded; exposed; expostulated; expounded; expressed; extolled.

F
faltered; finished; flashed; flirted; foretold; forged on; fretted; frowned; fumed.

G
gabbed; gabbled; gagged; gaggled; gasped; gave; gawped; gibed; giggled; glowered; got out; granted; grated; greeted; grieved; grinned; gritted out; groaned; growled; grumbled; grunted; guessed; guffawed; gulped; gurgled; gushed.

H
haggled; handed on; harped; hastened to add; hastened to say; hedged; hesitated; hinted; hissed; hollered; hooted; howled; hypothesized.

I
imitated; imparted; implied; implored; importuned; inclined; indicated; informed; inquired; insinuated; insisted; instructed; insulted; interjected;

interposed; interrogated; interrupted; intimated; intimidated; intoned; invited.

J

jabbered; jeered; jested; joked; joshed; judged; justified.

K – L

keened; kidded; lamented; laughed; lectured; leered; lied; lilted; lisped.

M

made known; made public; maintained; managed; marveled; mentioned; mewled; mimicked; moaned; mocked; mourned; mumbled; murmured; mused; muttered.

N – O

nagged; narrated; necessitated; nodded; noted; notified; objected; observed; offered; orated; ordered.

P

panted; passed on; perceived; persisted; persuaded; pestered; petitioned; piped; piped up; pleaded; pledged; pointed out; pondered; postulated; pouted; praised; prayed; preached; premised; presented; presupposed; prevaricated; proceeded; proclaimed; prodded; profaned; professed; proffered; promised; prompted; promulgated; pronounced; prophesied; proposed; protested; provoked; publicized; published; puled; purred; put forth; put in; put out; puzzled.

Q

quacked; quaked; qualified; quarreled; quavered; queried; questioned; quibbled; quipped; quivered; quizzed; quoted.

R

raged; railed; rambled; ranted; rattled off; reasoned; reassured; rebuffed; recalled; recanted; reckoned; recommended; reconciled; recounted; recriminated; refused; rejoiced; rejoined; related; released; remarked; remembered; reminded; remonstrated; repeated; replied; reported; reprimanded; reputed; requested; required; requisitioned; responded; restated; retorted; revealed; roared.

S

said; sang; sassed; scoffed; scolded; screamed; searched; seethed; sent on; settled; shared; shot; shot back; shouted; shrieked; shrilled; shrugged; shuddered; sighed; smiled; smirked; snapped; snarled; sneered; sneezed; snickered; sniffed; sniffled; sniveled; snorted; sobbed; solicited; sought; spat; spat out; specified; speculated; spluttered; spoke; sputtered; squeaked; stammered; started; stated; stormed; stressed; stuttered; suggested; supposed; surmised; swore.

T

taunted; teased; tempted; tested; testified; thanked (someone); theorized; threatened; threw back; thundered; told (someone); told off; touted; trailed off; transferred; transmitted; trembled; trilled; trumpeted; twanged; twittered.

U – V

urged; uttered; validated; ventured; verbalized; verified; vociferated; voiced; volunteered; vowed.

W

wailed; wangled; warbled; warned; went on; wept; wheedled; whimpered; whined; whispered; wondered; worried.

Y

yakked; yapped; yawned; yelled; yelped; yowled.

Emotion: Anger

accused; argued; barked; belittled; bellowed; berated; bit out; blasted; blasted back; blazed; blew up; boomed; bossed; bragged; broke in; bullied; burst out; called; called out; carped; cautioned; challenged; charged; chided; commanded; complained; condemned; confuted; cried; cried out; criticized; cursed; demanded; demurred; dinned; disrupted; exploded; expostulated; flashed; fumed; grated; gritted out; growled; grunted; hissed; hollered; howled; insinuated; insulted; intimidated; jeered; lectured; leered; lied; mocked; muttered; nagged; objected; persisted; preached; proclaimed; profaned; provoked; quarreled; raged; railed; rambled; ranted; remonstrated; reprimanded; retorted; roared; sassed; scoffed; scolded; screamed; seethed; shot; shot back; shouted; shrieked; shrilled; snapped; snarled; sneered; snorted; spat; spat out; squawked; stormed; swore; taunted; threatened; threw back; thundered; told off; vociferated; vowed; warned; yelled.

USAGE EXAMPLES

"He will never amount to anything," she *belittled*.

"Get over here this instant!" David *called*.

"I can't stand the sight of your face," Susan *grated*. "You're a sick little man!"

"I hate you!" she *seethed*.

"You're a liar!" he *yelled*. "I don't even know you."

Emotion: Fear

appealed; babbled; bawled; begged; beseeched; blubbered; burst out; called; called out; chattered; choked; choked out; cracked; cried; cried out; croaked; emitted; entreated; exclaimed; faltered; fretted; gagged; gasped; got out; gritted out; gulped; hesitated; hissed; howled; implored; managed; mewled; moaned; mumbled; murmured; muttered; petitioned; pleaded; prayed; puled; quaked; quavered; quivered; rambled; ranted; screamed; shrieked; shuddered; sobbed; spluttered; squeaked;

stammered; started; stuttered; trembled; wailed; warbled; wept; whimpered; whispered; worried; yelped; yowled.

USAGE EXAMPLES

"Please," she *called out*, "someone help me!"

"Are they still coming?" she *croaked*.

"I–I can't move," Kylie *faltered*.

"They're armed with knives," he *managed*.

"Mommy," the boy *squeaked*, "there's a ghost at the window."

Emotion: Happiness

babbled; bantered; beamed; bubbled; burst out; cackled; caroled; chanted; chatted; cheered; chortled; chuckled; congratulated; giggled; greeted; grinned; guffawed; gushed; hooted; jabbered; jested; joked; joshed; laughed; marveled; purred; rambled; rejoiced; sang; smiled; smirked; snickered; snorted; thanked (someone); yapped.

USAGE EXAMPLES

Carol *beamed*. "It's a boy!"

"You always say that." He *chuckled*.

"Are you ready to go?" She *grinned*.

"She is such a klutz." John *laughed*.

"I can't wait." She *smiled*.

Emotion: Love

announced; assured; babbled; bantered; beckoned; breathed; bubbled; cajoled; coaxed; comforted; confided; congratulated; consoled; cooed; counseled; craved; crooned; declared; doted; empathized; encouraged; giggled; greeted; grinned; groaned; gushed; invited; moaned; mused; persuaded; pledged; pouted; praised; proclaimed; professed; proposed; purred; rambled; reassured; rejoiced; sang; sassed; sighed; smiled; smirked; teased; tempted; urged; ventured; vowed.

USAGE EXAMPLES

"I need you," she *breathed.*

"Go to sleep, little one," the mother *cooed.*

"When are you coming over?" Jasmine *pouted.*

"I love you," he *professed.*

"We miss you here," she *sighed.*

Emotion: Sadness

agonized; appealed; argued; barked; bawled; bayed; begged; bellowed; bemoaned; bewailed; bickered; bleated; blubbered; carped; caviled; clamored; complained; cried; deplored; fussed; gagged; glowered; groaned; grouched; growled; grumbled; hissed; howled; keened; lamented; mewled; moaned; mourned; murmured; muttered; nagged; objected; protested; puled; quarreled; quetched; quibbled; roared; rued; screamed; screeched; shouted; shrieked; sighed; sniffed; sniffled; sniveled; sobbed; spat; spat out; squalled; squawked; squealed; threatened; trembled; ululated; wailed; wept; whimpered; whined; whinged; whispered; yammered; yelled; yelped.

USAGE EXAMPLES

"I have nothing left to live for." Cathy *bawled.*

"Why do we have to go?" her son *grumbled*.

"Are we there yet?" Michael *moaned*. "I'm sick of waiting."

"She told me everything!" she *shrieked*.

"You have nothing to offer me," he *hissed*. "Take your stuff and leave."

Emotion: Surprise

blurted; blurted out; breathed; burst out; called; called out; cried; cried out; exclaimed; faltered; gasped; gawped; gulped; hesitated; inquired; interjected; interrupted; marveled; objected; protested; puzzled; quaked; quavered; queried; questioned; quivered; quizzed; shouted; shrieked; shrilled; spat out; spluttered; sputtered; squeaked; stammered; started; stressed; stuttered; swore; trembled; trilled; trumpeted; worried; yelped; yowled.

USAGE EXAMPLES

"What the hell are you doing here?" he *exclaimed*.

"Oh, no!" Karen *gasped*.

"How is this possible?" she *puzzled*. "I thought you were dead."

"Y-you just appeared out of thin air," the man *spluttered*.

"Ah!" she *yelped*. "You scared me half to death."

Dynamics: Loud

barked; bawled; bellowed; blasted; blazed; blew up; boomed; called; called out; chanted; cheered; cried; cried out; crowed; dinned; exploded; hollered; hooted; howled; keened; mewled; raged; ranted; roared; screamed; shouted; shrieked; shrilled; stormed; thundered; trumpeted; wailed; whined; yelled; yelped; yowled.

USAGE EXAMPLES

"I know what you did!" she *barked*.

"Someone call the police," Mary *cried out*.

"Of course I'm right," he *exploded*.

"You better stay away from her!" *roared* James.

"Quick," he *shouted*, "he's over there by the river."

Dynamics: Soft

breathed; cooed; crooned; gasped; gawped; grinned; gulped; mumbled; murmured; muttered; nodded; purred; quivered; shrugged; shuddered; sighed; smiled; smirked; snarled; sneered; snickered; sniffed; sniffled; squeaked; trembled; twittered; whimpered; whispered; yawned.

USAGE EXAMPLES

"Darling," she *breathed*, "I'm leaving now."

"Hello, nice to meet you," Cathy *mumbled*.

"I'm sorry," she *murmured*. "I can't go with you."

"It's probably for the best," he *sighed*.

"Be quiet, or they will hear you," Nick *whispered*.

2
Dialogue Adverbs

Adverbs are used to modify verbs, adjectives, and other adverbs. When included alongside dialogue tags, adverbs can make written dialogue more expressive.

Adverbs in Alphabetical Order

A

abandonedly; abashedly; abhorrently; abidingly; abjectly; abrasively; abruptly; absentmindedly; absently; absorbedly; absorbingly; abstractly; abstrusely; absurdly; abusively; abysmally; academically; acceptingly; accessibly; accidentally; accommodatingly; accomplishedly; accurately; accusatively; accusatorily; accusingly; acerbically; achingly; acidly; acknowledgingly; acridly; acrimoniously; adamantly; adequately; admirably; admiringly; admonishingly; adorably; adoringly; adroitly; adventurously; adversarially; affably; affectedly; affectingly; affectionately; affirmatively; affirmingly; affrontedly; aggravatedly; aggravatingly; aggressively; aggrievedly; aghastly; agilely; agitatedly; agonizedly; agreeably; agreeingly; aimlessly; airily; alarmedly; alarmingly; alertly; allegorically; alliteratively; alludingly; alluringly; allusively; aloofly; aloud; altruistically; amateurishly; amatively; amazedly; ambiguously; ambitiously; ambivalently; amenably; amiably; amicably; amorally; amorously; amusedly; amusingly; analytically; anarchically; angelically; angrily; anguishedly; animalistically; animatedly; annoyedly; annoyingly; answeringly; antagonistically; anticlimatically; anticipatingly; anticipatorily; antipathetically; antisocially; anxiously; apathetically; apologetically; apoplectically; appealingly; appeasingly; appositely; appraisingly; appreciatively; apprehensibly; apprehensively; appropriately; approvingly; aptly; arbitrarily; arcanely; ardently; arduously; argumentatively; aridly; aristocratically; arousedly; arousingly; arrantly; arrogantly; artfully; articulately; ashamedly; asininely; assentingly; assertively; assessingly; assumingly; assuredly; assuringly; astonishedly; astoundedly;

astringently; astutely; attentively; attractively; atypically; audaciously; audibly; augustly; auspiciously; austerely; authoritatively; autocratically; automatically; autonomously; avariciously; avidly; awedly; awesomely; awestruckly; awfully; awkwardly.

B

back; backhandedly; bad-temperedly; badly; baffledly; bafflingly; balefully; ballistically; banally; banefully; banteringly; barbarically; barbarously; barefacedly; basely; bashfully; bawdily; beamingly; bearishly; beautifully; beckoningly; becomingly; befittingly; befuddledly; begrudgingly; beguilingly; belatedly; believably; believingly; bellicosely; belligerently; bemusedly; beneficently; beneficially; benevolently; benignantly; benignly; berserkly; beseechingly; besottedly; bestially; bewilderedly; bewilderingly; bewitchingly; biasedly; biliously; billowingly; bitchily; bitingly; bitterly; bittersweetly; bizarrely; blackly; blamelessly; blandly; blankly; blasphemously; blatantly; blazingly; bleakly; blindly; blissfully; blithely; blithesomely; bloodthirstily; bluffly; bluntly; blushingly; blusteringly; boastfully; boastingly; boilingly; boisterously; boldly; bombastically; bookishly; boomingly; boorishly; boozily; boredly; boringly; bossily; bouncily; boyishly; bracingly; braggingly; brashly; brassily; brattily; bravely; brazenly; breathily; breathlessly; breezily; briefly; bright-eyedly; brightly; brilliantly; briskly; brittlely; broken-heartedly; brokenly; broodingly; brusquely; brutally; brutishly; bubblingly; bullheadedly; bullyingly; bumblingly; burningly; busily.

C

cacophonously; caddishly; cagily; cajolingly; calculatingly; callously; callowly; calmingly; calmly; calumniously; candidly; cannily; cantankerously; capriciously; captiously; captivatedly; captivatingly; carefully; carelessly; caressingly; caringly; carnally; casually; casuistically; catatonically; cattily; caustically; cautiously; cavalierly; cavillously; censoriously; ceremonially; ceremoniously; chagrinedly; challengingly; chantingly; chaotically; characteristically; charily; charismatically; charitably; charmingly; chastely; chastenedly; chattily; chauvinistically; cheekily; cheerfully; cheerily; cheeringly; cheerlessly; cheesily; cherishedly; cherishingly; cherubically; chidingly; childishly; chillily; chillingly; chipperly; chirpily; chivalrously; chokingly; churlishly; circumspectly; civilly; clairvoyantly; clammily; clandestinely; clarifyingly; classily; classlessly; claustrophobically; clearly; cleverly;

clingingly; clinically; close-mindedly; cluelessly; clumsily; coarsely; coaxingly; cockily; cogently; cold-bloodedly; coldheartedly; coldly; collectedly; collectively; colorfully; colorlessly; coltishly; comatosely; combatively; comfortedly; comfortingly; comically; commandingly; commendatorily; commonly; compassionately; compellingly; compensatingly; competently; competitively; complacently; complainingly; complaisantly; complementarily; compliantly; complicitly; complimentarily; composedly; comprehendingly; compromisingly; compulsively; compulsorily; concedingly; conceitedly; concernedly; concertedly; conciliatorily; concisely; concludingly; conclusively; condemningly; condescendingly; conditionally; confidentially; confidently; confidingly; confirmingly; conflictedly; confoundedly; confrontationally; confusedly; confusingly; congenially; congestedly; congratulatorily; connivingly; conscientiously; consciously; consentingly; conservatively; considerately; consideringly; consolingly; conspicuously; conspiratorially; constrictedly; constructively; contemplatively; contemptibly; contemptuously; contentedly; contentiously; contently; continuingly; contradictorily; contrarily; contrastingly; contritely; contrivedly; controlledly; contumaciously; contumeliously; conversationally; convincingly; convivially; convolutely; convulsively; coolingly; coolly; cooperatively; coquettishly; cordially; correctedly; correctively; correctly; coughingly; counterproductively; courageously; courteously; covertly; covetously; cowardly; coyly; cozily; crabbily; craftily; crankily; crassly; cravenly; crazily; creakily; creamily; creatively; credulously; creepily; crescendingly; crestfallenly; cringingly; crisply; critically; croakily; croakingly; crossly; crudely; cruelly; crushedly; crushingly; crustily; cryptically; cultivatedly; culturedly; cunningly; curiously; cursorily; curtly; cutely; cuttingly; cynically.

D

daftly; daintily; damply; dangerously; dapperly; daringly; darkly; dashingly; dauntedly; dauntingly; dauntlessly; dazedly; dazzlingly; deadpan; deafeningly; dearly; debasedly; debasingly; debauchedly; debonairly; decadently; deceitfully; decently; deceptively; decidedly; decisively; decorously; deductively; deeply; defamatorily; defeatedly; defenselessly; defensively; deferentially; defiantly; definitely; deflatedly; deflectingly; deftly; dejectedly; delectably; deliberately; delicately; deliciously; delightedly; delightfully; deliriously; deludedly; demandingly; dementedly; demonstrably; demonstratively; demurely; densely; denunciatorily; denyingly; dependably; deplorably; depravedly;

deprecatingly; deprecatively; depressedly; depressingly; derangedly; derisively; derivatively; derogatively; descriptively; deservingly; desirously; desolately; despairingly; desperately; despisingly; despondently; despotically; destructively; desultorily; detachedly; determinedly; devastatedly; devastatingly; devilishly; deviously; devotedly; devotionally; devoutly; diabolically; dictatorily; didactically; difficultly; diffidently; dignifiedly; diligently; diminutively; dimly; dimwittedly; diplomatically; directly; direly; dirtily; disagreeably; disagreeingly; disappointedly; disappointingly; disapprovingly; disarmingly; disastrously; disbelievingly; discernibly; discerningly; discombobulatedly; discomfortingly; disconcertedly; disconcertingly; disconnectedly; disconsolately; discontentedly; discordantly; discouragedly; discouragingly; discourteously; discreetly; discretely; discretionally; discriminatingly; disdainfully; disenchantedly; disfavorably; disgracefully; disgruntledly; disgustedly; disgustingly; disharmoniously; disheartenedly; dishearteningly; dishonestly; dishonorably; disillusionedly; disingenuously; disinterestedly; disjointedly; dismayedly; dismayingly; dismissively; disobediently; disobligingly; disorientedly; disparagingly; dispassionately; dispiritedly; displeasedly; disquietedly; disquietingly; disquietly; disrespectfully; disruptively; dissatisfiedly; dissentingly; dissolutely; dissonantly; dissuasively; distantly; distastefully; distinctively; distinctly; distinguishedly; distractedly; distractingly; distraughtly; distressedly; distrustfully; distrustingly; disturbedly; disturbingly; ditzily; dizzily; dizzyingly; docilely; doggedly; dogmatically; dolefully; dolorously; dominantly; domineeringly; dotingly; doubtfully; doubtingly; doughtily; dourly; downcastly; downheartedly; downtroddenly; draconially; drainedly; dramatically; drawlingly; dreadfully; dreadingly; dreamily; drearily; drolly; droopily; drowsily; drunkenly; dry-eyedly; dryly/drily; dubiously; dulcetly; dully; dumbfoundedly; dumbly; duplicitously; duskily; dutifully.

E

eagerly; earnestly; ear-piercingly; ear-splittingly; easily; ebulliently; eccentrically; echoingly; ecstatically; edaciously; edgily; educationally; eerily; effeminately; effervescently; effetely; efficaciously; effortfully; effortlessly; effusively; egotistically; elaborately; elatedly; elegantly; eloquently; elusively; embarrassedly; embitteredly; emotionally; emotionlessly; empathetically; emphatically; emptily; enamoredly; enchantedly; enchantingly; encouragedly; encouragingly; endearingly; energetically; engagedly; engagingly; engrossedly; enigmatically;

enjoyably; enlightenedly; enormously; enquiringly; enragedly; enrapturedly; enterprisingly; entertainedly; entertainingly; enthralledly; enthrallingly; enthusedly; enthusiastically; enticingly; entrancedly; entrancingly; entreatingly; enviably; enviously; equivocally; erratically; erroneously; eruditely; esoterically; esuriently; ethereally; euphemistically; euphoniously; euphorically; evaluatingly; evanescently; evasively; evenly; eventually; evilly; evocatively; exacerbatedly; exactingly; exaggeratedly; exaltedly; exasperatedly; exasperatingly; execrably; excitedly; excitingly; excusingly; exhalingly; exhaustedly; exhaustively; exhilaratedly; exhilaratingly; exigently; exotically; expansively; expectantly; experiencedly; experimentally; expertly; explanatively; explicitly; exploratorily; explosively; expressionlessly; expressively; exquisitely; extemporaneously; extravagantly; exuberantly; exultantly; exultingly.

F

facetiously; facilely; factually; faintheartedly; faintly; fairly; faithfully; faithlessly; fallaciously; falsely; falteringly; familiarly; famishedly; fanatically; fancifully; fancily; fantastically; farcically; fascinatedly; fastidiously; fatalistically; fatefully; fatuously; favorably; fawningly; fearfully; fearlessly; fearsomely; fecklessly; feebly; feelingly; feignedly; felicitously; femininely; ferally; ferociously; fervently; fervidly; festively; fetchingly; fetidly; feudally; feverishly; fibbingly; ficklely; fiendishly; fiercely; figuratively; filially; filthily; finally; finickily; finickingly; firmly; fishily; fitfully; fittingly; fixatedly; fixedly; flabbergastedly; flagrantly; flakily; flamboyantly; flamingly; flashily; flashingly; flatly; flatteredly; flatteringly; flauntingly; flawlessly; fleetingly; flickeringly; flightily; flimsily; flippantly; flirtatiously; flirtingly; floridly; floutingly; flowingly; fluently; fluidly; flummoxedly; flushedly; flusteredly; flutteringly; foggily; fondly; foolishly; foppishly; forbearingly; forbiddingly; forcedly; forcefully; forcibly; forebodingly; foreignly; foreknowingly; foresakenly; foreseeingly; foresightedly; forgetfully; forgivingly; forlornly; formally; formidably; forthrightly; fortuitously; fortunately; forwardly; foulmouthedly; foully; foxily; fractiously; fragilely; frailly; frankly; frantically; fraudulently; frazzledly; freakishly; freezingly; frenetically; frenziedly; freshly; fretfully; friendlily; frightenedly; frighteningly; frightfully; frigidly; friskily; frivolously; frolicsomely; frostily; frowningly; frozenly; frugally; frustratedly; fulsomely; fumblingly; funereally; funnily; furiously; furtively; fussily; futilely.

G

gaily; gallantly; gallingly; galvanically; galvanizingly; gamely; garbledly; garishly; garrulously; gaspingly; gaudily; gawkishly; geekily; generously; genially; genteelly; gentlemanly; gently; genuinely; germanely; ghastfully; ghoulishly; giddily; gigantically; gigglingly; gingerly; girlishly; gladly; glamorously; glancingly; glaringly; glassily; gleefully; glibly; glintingly; glisteringly; glitteringly; gloatingly; gloomily; gloriously; glossily; gloweringly; glowingly; glumly; gluttonously; goadingly; good-humoredly; good-naturedly; goofily; gorgeously; gorily; gracefully; gracelessly; graciously; grandfatherly; grandiloquently; grandiosely; grandly; graphically; gratefully; gratifiedly; gratifyingly; gratingly; gratuitously; gravely; greasily; greedily; greenly; gregariously; grimly; grindingly; grinningly; grittily; groaningly; groggily; gropingly; grossly; grotesquely; grouchily; groundedly; groundlessly; grovelingly; growlingly; grudgingly; gruesomely; gruffly; grumblingly; grumpily; gruntingly; guardedly; guardingly; guessingly; guidingly; guilefully; guilelessly; guiltily; guiltlessly; gullibly; gurglingly; gushingly; gustily; gutsily; gutturally.

H

habitually; haggardly; hair-raisingly; halfheartedly; haltingly; hamfistedly; handily; handsomely; haphazardly; haplessly; happily; harassingly; hardheadedly; hardheartedly; hardly; harmfully; harmlessly; harmonically; harmoniously; harriedly; harrowingly; harshly; hastily; hatefully; haughtily; hauntedly; hauntingly; hawkishly; hazily; headily; heart-breakingly; heartbrokenly; heartenedly; hearteningly; heartfeltly; heartily; heartlessly; heartrendingly; heatedly; heavenly; heavily; heavy-handedly; heavy-heartedly; hectically; hedonistically; heedfully; heedlessly; heftily; heinously; hellishly; helpfully; helplessly; heraldically; heretically; heroically; hesitantly; hesitatingly; hiddenly; hideously; hilariously; hinderingly; hintingly; hissingly; historically; histrionically; hoarsely; hoggishly; hollowly; honestly; honorably; honoredly; honorifically; hopefully; hopelessly; hopingly; horribly; horridly; horrifically; horrifiedly; horrifyingly; hospitably; hostilely; hotheadedly; hotly; hubristically; huffily; hugely; huggingly; humanely; humbly; humiliatedly; humiliatingly; humorlessly; humorously; hungrily; hurriedly; hurtfully; hurtly; hushedly; huskily; hyperactively; hyperbolically; hypnotically; hypocritically; hypothetically; hysterically.

I

icily; idealistically; idiosyncratically; idiotically; idly; idolizingly; ignorantly; ill-humoredly; ill-naturedly; ill-temperedly; illiberally; illogically; illuminatedly; illustratively; imaginatively; imitatively; immaturely; immediately; immodestly; immovably; immutably; impalpably; impartially; impassively; impatiently; impeccably; impedingly; imperatively; imperceptibly; imperfectly; imperiously; impersonally; impertinently; imperturbably; impetuously; impiously; impishly; implacably; implausibly; implicitly; imploringly; impolitely; importantly; importunately; importunely; imposingly; impotently; imprecisely; impressedly; impressionably; impressively; improbably; improperly; improvisationally; imprudently; impudently; impulsively; inaccurately; inadequately; inadvertently; inanely; inappropriately; inaptly; inarticulately; inattentively; inaudibly; inauspiciously; incautiously; incessantly; inclusively; incoherently; incompetently; incompletely; incomprehendingly; incomprehensibly; inconceivably; inconclusively; incongrously; inconsequentially; inconsequently; inconsiderately; inconsistently; inconsolably; inconveniently; incorrectly; incorrigibly; incredibly; incredulously; incuriously; indebtedly; indecently; indecisively; indecorously; indelicately; independently; indeterminedly; indicatively; indifferently; indignantly; indirectly; indiscreetly; indiscriminately; indistinctly; indolently; indulgently; industriously; inebriatedly; ineffectively; ineffectually; inelegantly; ineloquently; ineptly; inevitably; inexactly; inexcusably; inexorably; inexperiencedly; inexpertly; inexplicably; inexpressively; infatuatedly; infectiously; inflexibly; influentially; informally; informatively; infuriatingly; ingeniously; ingenuously; ingratiatingly; inhalingly; inharmoniously; inhospitably; inhumanely; inhumanly; inimically; iniquitously; injudiciously; innocently; innocuously; inoffensively; inopportunely; inquiringly; inquisitively; insanely; insatiably; inscrutably; insensibly; insensitively; insidiously; insightfully; insignificantly; insincerely; insinuatingly; insipidly; insistently; insolently; insouciantly; inspiredly; inspiringly; instantaneously; instantly; instinctively; instinctually; instructively; insubordinately; insufferably; insufficiently; insultedly; insultingly; intelligently; intemperately; intensely; intentionally; intently; interestedly; interestingly; interminably; intermittently; interrogatively; intimately; intimidatedly; intimidatingly; intolerantly; intoxicatedly; intoxicatingly; intractably; intransigently; intrepidly; intricately; intriguedly; intriguingly; introductorily; introspectively; introvertedly; intrusively; intuitively; invasively; invectively; inventively; invigoratedly; invigoratingly; invitingly; involuntarily; inwardly; irascibly; irately;

irefully; irenically; irksomely; ironhandedly; ironically; irrationally; irregularly; irrelevantly; irrepressibly; irresistibly; irresolutely; irresponsibly; irreverently; irrevocably; irritably; irritatedly; irritatingly; itchily.

J

jadedly; jaggedly; jarringly; jauntily; jazzily; jealously; jeeringly; jejunely; jerkily; jestingly; jocosely; jocularly; jointly; jokingly; jollily; joltingly; joshingly; jovially; joyfully; joylessly; joyously; jubilantly; judgmentally; judiciously; juicily; jumpily; justifiedly; justly.

K

keenly; kiddingly; kindheartedly; kindly; kinkily; knavishly; knottily; knowingly; knowledgeably; kookily.

L

laboredly; laboriously; lachrymosely; lackadaisically; lacklusterly; laconically; ladylike; lamely; lamentingly; languidly; languishingly; languorously; lasciviously; lauditorily; laughingly; lavishly; laxly; lazily; leadenly; leadingly; learnedly; lecherously; leerily; leeringly; legalistically; leisurely; lengthily; leniently; lethally; lethargically; levelly; lewdly; libelously; libidinously; licentiously; lifelessly; lightheadedly; lightheartedly; lightly; liltingly; limpidly; limply; lingeringly; lispily; lispingly; listlessly; literally; lividly; loathingly; loftily; logically; lonesomely; long-sufferingly; long-windedly; longingly; loosely; loquaciously; loudly; lousily; lovingly; loyally; lucidly; ludicrously; lugubriously; lumberingly; luminously; luridly; lushly; lustfully; lustily; luxuriously; lyrically.

M

macabrely; maddeningly; madly; magisterially; magnanimously; magnificently; magniloquently; majestically; malevolently; maliciously; malignantly; manfully; maniacally; manically; manipulatively; mannerly; mannishly; markedly; martially; marvelously; masculinely; masochistically; massively; masterfully; materialistically; maternally; matronly; matter-of-factly; maturely; mawkishly; mean-spiritedly; meanderingly; meaningfully; meaninglessly; meanly; measuredly;

measuringly; mechanically; meddlesomely; meditatively; meekly; melancholically; mellifluously; mellowly; melodically; melodiously; melodramatically; memorisingly; menacingly; mendaciously; mentally; mercifully; mercilessly; mercurially; merrily; mesmerizedly; mesmerizingly; messily; metallically; metaphorically; methodically; meticulously; mightily; mild-manneredly; mildly; militantly; militaristically; mimickingly; minaciously; mincingly; mindfully; mindlessly; mindnumbingly; mirthfully; mirthlessly; mischievously; miserably; misgivingly; misguidedly; misguidingly; misleadingly; mistakenly; mistily; mistrustfully; mistrustingly; mockingly; moderately; modestly; moistly; momentously; monosyllabically; monotonously; monstrously; moodily; mopingly; morally; morbidly; mordaciously; mordantly; moronically; morosely; mortifiedly; motheringly; motionlessly; motivatedly; mournfully; mousily; movingly; muddledly; muffledly; mulishly; mullishly; mumblingly; mundanely; munificently; murderously; murkily; murmuringly; mushily; musically; musingly; mutedly; mutely; mutinously; mutteringly; mysteriously; mystically; mystifiedly.

N

naggingly; naively; narcissistically; narrow-eyedly; narrow-mindedly; nasally; nastily; natively; nattily; naturally; naughtily; nauseatingly; nauseously; nebulously; needfully; needily; needingly; needlessly; nefariously; negatively; neglectedly; neglectfully; negligently; nervelessly; nervously; neurotically; neutrally; nicely; niggardly; nigglingly; nimbly; nobly; noddingly; noiselessly; noisily; noisomely; nonchalantly; noncommittally; noncompetitively; noncompliantly; nonjudgmentally; nonplussedly; nonsensically; nonverbally; nosily; nostalgically; notably; noxiously; numbly; nuttily.

O

oafishly; obdurately; obediently; obeisantly; objectively; obligatorily; obligedly; obligingly; obliquely; obliviously; obnoxiously; obscenely; obscurely; obsequiously; observantly; obsessively; obstinately; obstreperously; obtrusively; obtusely; occupiedly; oddly; odorously; offendedly; offensively; offhandedly; officially; officiously; oilily; ominously; onerously; open-mindedly; open-mouthedly; openhandedly; openly; opinionatedly; opportunely; opportunistically; opposedly; oppositely; oppressively; opprobriously; optimistically; oracularly; orderingly; ostensibly; ostentatiously; outlandishly; outragedly;

outrageously; outrightly; outspokenly; over-enthusiastically; overbearingly; overconfidently; overeagerly; overjoyedly; overprotectively; overtly; overwhelmedly; overwhelmingly; overzealously; owlishly; oxymoronically.

P

painedly; painfully; painlessly; painstakingly; palely; pallidly; panickingly; pantingly; paradoxically; paranoidly; parenthetically; parochially; parsimoniously; partially; partingly; passingly; passionately; passionlessly; passively; paternally; pathetically; patiently; patriarchally; patriotically; patronizingly; pausingly; peaceably; peacefully; peculiarly; pedantically; peevedly; peevishly; pejoratively; pellucidly; penetratingly; penitentially; penitently; pensively; perceptibly; perceptively; peremptorily; perfectly; perfidiously; perfunctorily; perkily; permissively; perplexedly; perseveringly; persistently; perspicaciously; perspicuously; perspiringly; persuadedly; persuasively; pertinaciously; pertinently; pertly; perturbedly; perversely; pervertedly; pessimistically; pesteringly; pestiferously; petrifiedly; pettishly; petulantly; philosophically; phlegmatically; pickily; picturesquely; piercingly; pietistically; piggishly; pigheadedly; piously; piquantly; piteously; pithily; pitifully; pitilessly; pityingly; placatingly; placidly; plainly; plaintively; plangently; platitudinously; platonically; plausibly; playfully; pleadingly; pleasantly; pleasedly; pleasingly; pleasurably; pliantly; pluckily; poetically; poignantly; pointblank; pointedly; pointlessly; poisedly; poisonously; pokingly; polishedly; politely; politically; pompously; ponderingly; ponderously; pontifically; poorly; portentously; positively; possessively; potently; poutily; powerfully; powerlessly; practically; pragmatically; prayerfully; pre-emptively; precariously; preciously; precipitately; precipitously; precisely; precociously; precognizantly; predatorily; predictably; predictively; preferentially; prejudgementally; prejudicedly; prematurely; preoccupiedly; preparatorily; preparedly; preposterously; pressingly; pressuringly; presumingly; presumptively; presumptuously; pretentiously; prettily; preventively; pridefully; priggishly; primitively; primly; prissily; pristinely; proactively; probingly; proddingly; prodigally; profanely; professionally; proficiently; profligately; profoundly; profusely; prognostically; prognosticatively; progressively; prohibitively; prolifically; promiscuously; promisingly; promptingly; promptly; prophetically; propitiatingly; propitiously; proprietarily; prosaically; prosily; prospectively; protectively; protestingly; protractedly; proudly; providently; provisionally; provocatively; prudently; prudishly;

pruriently; pryingly; puckishly; puerilely; puffily; pugnaciously; puissantly; punctiliously; punctually; pungently; punishingly; punitively; puppyishly; puritanically; purposefully; purposelessly; pushily; pusillanimously; putridly; puzzledly.

Q

quaintly; quakingly; quarrelsomely; quaveringly; queasily; queerly; quellingly; querulously; queryingly; questionably; questioningly; quickly; quiescently; quietly; quirkily; quiveringly; quixotically; quizzically.

R

rabidly; racily; radiantly; raggedly; ragingly; railingly; rakishly; ramblingly; rambunctiously; rancidly; rancorously; randily; randomly; rankly; rantingly; rapaciously; rapidly; raptly; rapturously; rashly; raspily; raspingly; rationally; rattlingly; raucously; raunchily; ravenously; ravishingly; readily; realistically; realizingly; reasonably; reasonlessly; reassuredly; reassuringly; rebelliously; rebukingly; recalcitrantly; receptively; reciprocatively; recklessly; reclusively; recollectively; red-facedly; red-handedly; reddeningly; redundantly; reelingly; refinedly; reflectively; reflexively; refractorily; refreshedly; refreshingly; regally; regardfully; regardlessly; regretfully; reinforcingly; rejectedly; rejoicingly; relaxedly; relaxingly; relentingly; relentlessly; relevantly; reliably; relievedly; relievingly; religiously; relishingly; reluctantly; remarkably; remedially; rememberingly; reminiscently; remonstrantly; remorsefully; remorselessly; remotely; repeatedly; repellently; repentantly; repetitiously; repetitively; reprehensively; reprimandingly; reproachfully; reprovingly; repulsedly; repulsively; resentfully; reservedly; resignedly; resolutely; resolvedly; resonantly; resoundingly; respectably; respectfully; respectively; resplendently; responsibly; responsively; restfully; restively; restlessly; restrainedly; restrainingly; restrictedly; restrictively; retaliatingly; reticently; retractively; retributively; retroactively; retrospectively; revealingly; revengefully; reverberantly; reverently; revoltingly; revolutionarily; rewardingly; rhapsodically; rhetorically; rhythmically; rhythmlessly; riantly; ribaldly; ridiculously; righteously; rightfully; rigidly; rigorously; ringingly; riotously; ripely; risibly; riskily; risquély; ritualistically; ritually; robustly; roguishly; roisterously; rollickingly; romantically; rosily; rottenly; roughly; rousingly; routinely; rowdily; royally; rudely; ruefully; ruggedly; rumblingly; ruminatingly; ruminatively; rustily; ruthlessly.

S

sacrilegiously; saddenedly; sadistically; sadly; sagaciously; sagely; salaciously; saltily; salutatorily; sanctimoniously; sanely; sanguinely; sappily; sarcastically; sardonically; sassily; satirically; satisfactorily; satisfiedly; satisfyingly; saturninely; saucily; savagely; savoringly; savvily; scandalously; scaredly; scarily; scathingly; schemingly; scholastically; scientifically; scintillatingly; scoffingly; scoldedly; scoldingly; scorchingly; scornedly; scornfully; scowlingly; scratchily; scrupulously; scurrilously; searchingly; searingly; secretively; sedately; seditiously; seductively; sedulously; seekingly; seethingly; self-absorbedly; self-approvingly; self-assuredly; self-centeredly; self-confidently; self-consciously; self-critically; self-deprecatingly; self-effacingly; self-importantly; self-indulgently; self-interestedly; self-mockingly; self-pityingly; self-possessedly; self-righteously; self-satisfiedly; self-servingly; selfishly; selflessly; senselessly; sensibly; sensitively; sensually; sensuously; sententiously; sentimentally; separately; sepulchrally; serendipitously; serenely; seriously; servilely; severely; sexily; shakenly; shakily; shakingly; shallowly; shamefacedly; shamefully; shamelessly; sharply; shatteringly; sheepishly; shiftily; shiftingly; shiveringly; shockedly; shockingly; short-temperedly; shortly; showily; shrewdly; shrewishly; shrilly; shrinkingly; shudderingly; shyly; sibilantly; sickeningly; sickly; sighingly; significantly; silkily; sillily; simperingly; simplistically; simply; simultaneously; sincerely; sinfully; singingly; singlemindedly; sinisterly; skeptically; sketchily; skillfully; skittishly; slackly; slanderously; slavishly; sleekly; sleepily; slickly; slimily; slipperily; slobberingly; sloppily; slothfully; slowly; sluggishly; slurringly; sluttishly; slyly; smarmily; smartly; smilingly; smirkingly; smokily; smolderingly; smoothly; smotheringly; smugly; smuttily; snappily; sneakily; sneeringly; snidely; sniffily; snobbily; snobbishly; snootily; sobbingly; soberly; sociably; soddenly; softheartedly; softly; solemnly; solicitously; solidly; somberly; somnolently; sonorously; soothedly; soothingly; sophisticatedly; soporifically; sordidly; sorely; sorrowfully; soulfully; sourly; speciously; speculatively; speechlessly; speedily; spellbindingly; spellbound; spicily; spinelessly; spiritedly; spiritlessly; spiritually; spitefully; splenetically; spoiledly; spontaneously; spookily; sporadically; sportily; spunkily; squarely; squeakily; squeamishly; stably; staidly; stalely; stalwartly; stammeringly; standoffishly; starchily; starkly; startledly; startlingly; staunchly; steadfastly; steadily; steadyingly; stealthily; steamily; steelily; sternly; stiffly; stifledly; stiflingly; stiltedly; stingily; stingingly; stoically; stolidly; stonily; stormily; stoutly; straightfacedly; strainedly; strainingly; strangely; strangledly; strategically; strenuously; strepitously; stressedly;

stressfully; strictly; stridently; strikingly; stringently; strongly; stubbornly; studiously; stuffily; stumblingly; stumpedly; stunnedly; stupefiedly; stupidly; stuporously; sturdily; stutteringly; stylishly; suavely; subduedly; subjectively; submissively; subserviently; subtly; subversively; succinctly; suddenly; sufferingly; suffocatingly; suggestingly; suggestively; sulkily; sullenly; sultrily; sunnily; superciliously; superficially; superfluously; superiorily; superstitiously; suppliantly; supplicatingly; supportedly; supportively; surlily; surprisedly; surprisingly; surreally; surrenderingly; surreptitiously; suspectingly; suspensefully; suspiciously; swaggeringly; sweetly; swiftly; sycophantically; symbolically; sympathetically; systematically.

T

taciturnly; tactfully; tactically; tactilely; tactlessly; tactually; talkatively; tamely; tantalizingly; tardily; tartly; tastefully; tastelessly; tauntingly; tautly; tearfully; tearily; teasingly; tediously; tellingly; temerariously; temperamentally; temperately; tempestuously; temptedly; temptingly; tenaciously; tenderly; tensely; tentatively; tenuously; tepidly; terribly; terrifiedly; terrifyingly; territorially; tersely; testily; testingly; tetchily; thankfully; thanklessly; theatrically; theoretically; therapeutically; thickheadedly; thickly; thinly; thirstily; thornily; thoughtfully; thoughtlessly; threatenedly; threateningly; thriftily; thrillingly; throatily; throbbingly; thuggishly; thumpingly; thunderingly; thunderously; thusly; tidily; tightly; timidly; timorously; tinglingly; tipsily; tiredly; tirelessly; tiresomely; tiringly; tolerantly; tomboyishly; tonelessly; toothily; toothlessly; topically; tormentedly; tormentingly; tornly; torpidly; torridly; torturously; touchily; touchingly; toughly; toxically; tragically; trailingly; traitorously; tranquilly; transfixedly; traumatically; treacherously; treasonably; treasonously; tremblingly; tremulously; trenchantly; trepidly; trickily; trillingly; trimly; tritely; triumphantly; troubledly; truculently; trustingly; trustworthily; truthfully; tumidly; tumultuously; tunefully; tunelessly; turbulently; turgidly; twangily; twinklingly; twistedly; twitchily; twitchingly; tyrannically.

U

uglily; unabashedly; unaffectedly; unaggressively; unambitiously; unamiably; unamicably; unamusedly; unapologetically; unappreciatively; unashamedly; unassumingly; unattractively; unbecomingly; unbelievingly; unbelligerently; unbendingly; unbiasedly; unblinkingly; unblushingly; uncannily; uncaringly; unceremoniously; uncertainly;

uncharacteristically; uncharitably; unchastely; uncheerfully; unchivalrously; uncivilly; unclearly; uncleverly; uncomfortably; uncommunicatively; uncompetitively; uncomplainingly; uncompliantly; uncomprehendingly; uncompromisingly; unconcernedly; unconsciously; unconsolably; uncontrollably; unconvincedly; unconvincingly; uncooperatively; uncordially; uncourageously; uncouthly; uncritically; unctuously; undauntedly; undecidedly; undecipherably; undefeatedly; underhandedly; understandably; understandingly; understatedly; undeservingly; undignifiedly; undistractedly; undividedly; uneasily; unemotionally; unenlightenedly; unenthusiastically; unenviously; unequivocally; unerringly; unethically; unevenly; unexpectedly; unfairly; unfaithfully; unfalteringly; unfamiliarly; unfashionably; unfavorably; unfazedly; unfearingly; unfeelingly; unflickeringly; unflinchingly; unfocusedly; unforgivingly; ungallantly; ungenerously; ungenially; unglamorously; ungraciously; ungratefully; ungrudgingly; unguardedly; unguiltily; unhaltingly; unhappily; unharmoniously; unheedingly; unhelpfully; unheroically; unhesitantly; unhesitatingly; unhurriedly; unimaginatively; unimposingly; unimpressedly; unimpressively; unindulgently; uninformatively; uninhibitedly; uninquisitively; uninspiredly; unintelligently; unintelligibly; unintentionally; uninterestedly; uninvitingly; unkindly; unknowingly; unmelodiously; unmercifully; unmindfully; unmotivatedly; unmovingly; unnecessarily; unnervedly; unnervingly; unobservantly; unobtrusively; unofficially; unostentatiously; unperturbedly; unpleasantly; unpoetically; unprecedentedly; unpredictably; unpreparedly; unpretentiously; unproductively; unprofessionally; unquestioningly; unrealistically; unreasonably; unreceptively; unrefinedly; unregretfully; unrelentingly; unreluctantly; unremorsefully; unrepentantly; unreservedly; unresponsively; unrestrainedly; unrevealingly; unromantically; unruffledly; unsatisfiedly; unscrupulously; unselfconsciously; unselfishly; unsettledly; unsettlingly; unshakably; unsmilingly; unsociably; unsolicitously; unsteadily; unsubtly; unsuccessfully; unsurely; unsurprisedly; unsurprisingly; unsuspectingly; unsympathetically; unthinkingly; unthreateningly; untrustingly; untruthfully; unvirtuously; unwantedly; unwarily; unwaveringly; unwelcomingly; unwillingly; unwisely; unyieldingly; upliftingly; uproariously; upsetly; urbanely; urgently; usefully; uselessly; uxoriously.

V

vacantly; vacillatingly; vacuously; vaguely; vaingloriously; vainly; valiantly; validly; valorously; vapidly; vauntingly; vehemently; venally;

venerably; veneratively; vengefully; venomously; venturesomely; veraciously; verbatim; verbosely; veritably; vexedly; vibrantly; vibratingly; vicariously; viciously; victoriously; vigilantly; vigorously; vilely; villainously; vindicatedly; vindictively; violently; virginally; virtuously; virulently; viscously; vitriolically; vituperatively; vivaciously; vividly; vocally; vociferously; voicelessly; volatilely; voluminously; voluntarily; voluptuously; voraciously; voyeuristically; vulgarly; vulnerably; vyingly.

W
waggishly; waifishly; wanderingly; wanly; wantingly; wantonly; warily; warmly; warningly; waspishly; watchfully; waveringly; waywardly; weakly; wearily; wearisomely; weepily; weightily; weirdly; welcomingly; well-meaningly; well-timedly; wetly; wheedlingly; wheezingly; whimperingly; whimsically; whinily; whiningly; whisperingly; wholeheartedly; wickedly; wide-eyedly; wildly; wilfully; wilily; willfully; willingly; wimpily; wimpishly; wincingly; windedly; winningly; winsomely; wintrily; wisely; wishfully; wispily; wistfully; witheringly; witlessly; wittily; wittingly; wobbily; woefully; wolfishly; wonderfully; wonderingly; wondrously; woodenly; woozily; wordily; wordlessly; worriedly; worrisomely; worshipfully; worshippingly; worthlessly; woundedly; wrathfully; wrenchingly; wretchedly; wrongly; wryly.

X – Y
xenophobically; yawningly; yearningly; yieldingly; yobbishly; youthfully.

Z
zanily; zealously; zestfully; zestily.

Emotion: Anger

abrasively; abusively; accusatively; accusingly; acidly; acridly; acrimoniously; aggressively; agitatedly; angrily; animalistically; antagonistically; antipathetically; apoplectically; argumentatively; arrogantly; astringently; bad-temperedly; ballistically; balefully; banefully; barbarically; barbarously; barefacedly; basely; bearishly; bellicosely; belligerently; beratingly; berserkly; bestially; biliously; billowingly; bitchily; bitingly; bitterly; blackly; blazingly; blusteringly; boastfully; boilingly; boldly; boomingly; bossily; brattily; briskly; brutally; brutishly; bullyingly; burningly; callously; calmly; cantankerously; captiously; cattily; caustically; chaotically; cheerlessly; chillingly; cholerically; churlishly; coarsely; cold-bloodedly; coldheartedly; coldly; combatively; condemningly; confrontationally; contemptuously; contentiously; contrarily; contumaciously; contumeliously; crabbily; crankily; critically; crossly; cruelly; crustily; cuttingly; cynically; dangerously; darkly; defiantly; demandingly; dementedly; deliberately; depravedly; derangedly; derisively; derogatively; despisingly; destructively; devilishly; diabolically; dictatorily; disapprovingly; disdainfully; disgruntledly; disputatiously; dissonantly; dominantly; domineeringly; dourly; draconially; drily; dyspeptically; edgily; enragedly; evilly; exacerbatedly; exactingly; exasperatedly; exasperatingly; explosively; fearsomely; ferally; ferociously; fervidly; feudally; fiercely; flamingly; floutingly; forcefully; foully; fractiously; frankly; frantically; frenetically; frenziedly; fretfully; frigidly; frustratedly; fumingly; furiously; gallingly; glacially; glassily; gloomily; goadingly; grouchily; growlingly; grudgingly; gruffly; grumpily; gruntingly; hamfistedly; harassingly; hardheartedly; hardly; harmfully; harriedly; harshly; hastily; hatefully; heartlessly; heatedly; heavy-handedly; heinously; hellishly; hideously; hissingly; horribly; hostilely; hotheadedly; hotly; huffily; humiliatingly; hurtfully; hypocritically; icily; ill-temperedly; indignantly; ingeniously; infuriatedly; iniquitously; insanely; insensitively; insidiously; insolently; insubordinately; intensely; intolerantly; invectively; irascibly; irately; irefully; ironhandedly; irritably; lividly; loudly; madly; malevolently; maliciously; malignantly; maniacally; masochistically; matter-of-factly; meanly; mean-spiritedly; menacingly; mercilessly; minaciously; mockingly; monstrously; mordantly; murderously; mutinously; negatively; noxiously; obdurately; obnoxiously; ominously; opprobriously; outragedly; peevishly; pejoratively; pertinaciously; perversely; pessimistically; pettishly; petulantly; pitilessly; poisonously; potently; powerfully; predatorily; primitively; pugnaciously;

punishingly; pushily; putridly; quarrelsomely; querulously; rabidly; ragingly; rancorously; rantingly; rapidly; rashly; recklessly; refractorily; remorselessly; reprochfully; resentfully; retaliatingly; revengefully; ribaldly; roughly; rudely; rumblingly; ruthlessly; sadistically; sarcastically; sardonically; savagely; scathingly; scoldingly; scorchingly; scornfully; scowlingly; scurrilously; searingly; seethingly; selfishly; seriously; severely; sharply; shatteringly; shrilly; slanderously; smolderingly; sneeringly; somberly; sorely; soullessly; sourly; spiritedly; spitefully; splenetically; spoiledly; sternly; stingingly; stormily; stringently; stubbornly; sulkily; temerariously; tensely; tersely; terrifyingly; territorially; testily; tetchily; thornily; threateningly; thuggishly; thunderingly; thunderously; tormentingly; toughly; toxically; truculently; tumultuously; turbulently; twistedly; tyrannically; uglily; unamusedly; unapologetically; unfeelingly; unkindly; unmercifully; unpleasantly; unsmilingly; vengefully; venomously; vexedly; viciously; victoriously; vilely; villainously; vindictively; violently; virulently; vitriolically; vituperatively; vociferously; volatilely; vulgarly; waspishly; wildly; wolfishly; wrathfully.

USAGE EXAMPLES

"You're dead!" she cursed *fiercely*.

"Do you miss your ex-husband?" Donald asked, *maliciously*.

"Billy," his father ordered *reproachfully*, "get over there in the corner!"

"There's nothing you can say," he hissed *resentfully*. "Now, get out of my sight!"

"I want you to suffer like I did!" she screamed *savagely*.

Emotion: Fear

agitatedly; alertly; anxiously; apprehensively; awkwardly; breathlessly; carefully; cautiously; circumspectly; cowardly; coweringly; croakily; despairingly; distrustfully; doubtfully; emotionally; faintheartedly; faintly; fearfully; feebly; fitfully; fragilely; frailly; frightenedly; fumblingly; gingerly; guardedly; gutlessly; haggardly; heedfully; hesitantly; hoarsely; huskily; hysterically; ineffectually; intimidatedly;

irrationally; jerkily; jitterily; jumpily; laboriously; nervously; neurotically; painstakingly; panically; panickingly; pantingly; paranoidly; perturbedly; petrifiedly; piteously; pithlessly; pusillanimously; quakingly; quaveringly; queasily; quietly; quiveringly; rabidly; raggedly; ramblingly; raspily; raspingly; reservedly; scaredly; scratchily; shakily; shrinkingly; shyly; skittishly; softly; spinelessly; spiritlessly; squeamishly; submissively; suspiciously; tautly; tearfully; tensely; tentatively; timidly; timorously; tormentedly; tremblingly; trepidatiously; trepidly; unassuredly; uncontrollably; uneasily; unnervedly; vigilantly; vulnerably; warily; watchfully; waveringly; weakly; whimperingly; wimpily; wimpishly; wobbily; xenophobically.

USAGE EXAMPLES

"Supposing someone should see us," she said *anxiously*.

Coweringly, Ben said, "Stay away from me."

"What was that sound?" Nancy whimpered *frightenedly*.

"Whatever it was, it was big," he said *shakily*.

"There's a man over there staring at us," the boy whispered *uneasily*.

Emotion: Happiness

admiringly; adoringly; adventurously; affectedly; amusedly; amusingly; animatedly; avidly; beamingly; bemusedly; blissfully; blithely; blithesomely; brightly; bubblingly; captivatedly; captivatingly; casually; charismatically; charmingly; chattily; cheekily; cheerfully; cheerily; cheeringly; chipperly; chirpily; congenially; congratulatorily; contentedly; contently; convivially; delightedly; delightfully; dreamily; eagerly; ebulliently; ecstatically; effervescently; effusively; elatedly; enamoredly; enchantedly; enchantingly; encouragedly; encouragingly; endearingly; energetically; engagedly; engagingly; enjoyably; enrapturedly; entertainedly; entertainingly; enthralledly; enthrallingly; enthusedly; enthusiastically; entrancedly; entrancingly; euphoniously; euphorically; exaltedly; excitedly; excitingly; exhilaratedly; exhilaratingly; expectantly; expressively; exuberantly; exultantly; exultingly; festively; frolicsomely; funnily; gaily; genially; genuinely;

giddily; gigglingly; gladly; gleefully; glisteringly; glitteringly; gloriously; glowingly; good-humoredly; good-naturedly; goofily; gratefully; gratifiedly; gratifyingly; gregariously; grinningly; gushingly; happily; harmoniously; heartily; hilariously; humorously; hyperactively; hysterically; infectiously; ingratiatingly; inspiredly; inspiringly; invigoratedly; invigoratingly; invitingly; irenically; irrepressibly; jauntily; jazzily; jestingly; jocosely; jocularly; jokingly; jollily; joshingly; jovially; joyfully; joyously; jubilantly; keenly; kiddingly; kookily; laughingly; leisurely; lightheartedly; liltingly; loquaciously; marvelously; mellifluously; melodiously; merrily; mirthfully; momentously; musically; nicely; over-enthusiastically; overeagerly; overjoyedly; overzealously; peacefully; perkily; piquantly; placidly; playfully; pleasantly; pleasedly; pleasingly; positively; quirkily; radiantly; rapturously; receptively; rejoicingly; relaxedly; relishingly; resplendently; responsively; rhapsodically; riantly; risibly; rollickingly; sanguinely; serenely; sillily; smilingly; smirkingly; sunnily; swaggeringly; talkatively; thrillingly; tinglingly; toothily; tranquilly; trickily; triumphantly; tunefully; twinklingly; uproariously; vibrantly; vibratingly; victoriously; vigorously; vivaciously; vividly; vocally; voraciously; waggishly; warmly; welcomingly; wholeheartedly; winningly; winsomely; wonderfully; youthfully; zanily; zealously; zestfully; zestily.

USAGE EXAMPLES

"Did you see his expression?" she said *amusedly*.

"Let's get this party started," Judy said *cheerfully*.

"Happy new year!" they yelled *festively*.

"Merry Christmas, dear boy!" Santa laughed *jovially*.

"It's time for dessert," she sang *tunefully* from the kitchen.

Emotion: Love

admirably; admiringly; adorably; adoringly; affectedly; affectingly; affectionately; alluringly; altruistically; amatively; amorously; appreciatively; arousedly; arousingly; attractively; bashfully;

beckoningly; becomingly; beneficently; benevolently; benignantly; benignly; besottedly; bewitchingly; blamelessly; blissfully; blushingly; captivatedly; captivatingly; caressingly; caringly; carnally; charismatically; charmingly; cheekily; cherishedly; cherishingly; chivalrously; clingingly; compassionately; concernedly; confidingly; considerately; consolingly; coquettishly; coyly; cozily; cutely; dashingly; dearly; debonairly; desirously; desperately; devotedly; devotionally; emotionally; empathetically; enamoredly; enchantedly; enchantingly; endearingly; enrapturedly; enticingly; entrancedly; entrancingly; faithfully; fawningly; feelingly; flatteringly; flirtatiously; flirtingly; fondly; forlornly; friendlily; friskily; giddily; girlishly; glowingly; good-naturedly; grandfatherly; gratefully; gratifiedly; gushingly; harmoniously; heartfeltly; heartily; helpfully; huggingly; humanely; infatuatedly; intimately; irresistibly; kindheartedly; kindly; kinkily; licentiously; longingly; loyally; lustfully; lustily; mesmerizedly; mesmerizingly; mildly; motheringly; munificently; mushily; needfully; needily; needingly; nicely; passionately; peaceably; peacefully; playfully; pleasantly; pleasedly; pleasingly; positively; possessively; poutily; preciously; prettily; promiscuously; protectively; randily; rapturously; raunchily; ravishingly; regardfully; romantically; sappily; seductively; selflessly; sensitively; sensually; sensuously; sentimentally; sexily; sincerely; smotheringly; softheartedly; soothedly; soothingly; soulfully; spellbindingly; supportedly; supportively; sweetly; sympathetically; teasingly; tempestuously; temptedly; temptingly; thankfully; understandingly; voluptuously; warmly; welcomingly; well-meaningly; wonderfully; worshipfully; worshippingly.

USAGE EXAMPLES

"He's the perfect man," she said *admiringly*.

"You're my hero," Kylie said *affectionately*.

"Mum," he said, *caringly*, "this house is for you."

"If only he would notice me," she mused *forlornly*.

"Come to bed," she purred *seductively*.

Emotion: Sadness

abandonedly; abysmally; achingly; aggrievedly; agonizedly; aimlessly; anguishedly; beseechingly; bitterly; blackly; bleakly; brittlely; broken-heartedly; brokenly; broodingly; chagrinedly; cheerlessly; chokingly; colorlessly; crestfallenly; crushedly; cynically; damply; darkly; dauntedly; defeatedly; deflatedly; dejectedly; depressedly; depressingly; desolately; despairingly; desperately; despondently; devastatedly; devastatingly; difficultly; direly; disappointedly; disappointingly; discomfortingly; disconcertedly; disconcertingly; discontentedly; discordantly; discouragedly; disenchantedly; disharmoniously; disheartenedly; dishearteningly; dismayedly; dismayingly; dispiritedly; displeasedly; dissatisfiedly; distantly; distraughtly; distressedly; disturbedly; dolefully; dolorously; dourly; downcastly; downheartedly; downtroddenly; dreadingly; drearily; droopily; duskily; emotionally; emptily; entreatingly; erratically; faithlessly; fatalistically; feebly; foresakenly; forlornly; fragilely; frailly; frowningly; futilely; gloomily; glumly; grimly; groaningly; grovelingly; grumblingly; haplessly; harriedly; hauntedly; heart-breakingly; heartbrokenly; heartrendingly; heavy-heartedly; helplessly; hoarsely; hollowly; hopelessly; humiliatedly; hurtly; imploringly; irrationally; irrepressibly; joylessly; laboredly; lachrymosely; lamentingly; languishingly; lonesomely; long-sufferingly; longingly; lugubriously; mawkishly; melancholically; melodramatically; mirthlessly; miserably; moodily; mopingly; morbidly; mournfully; negatively; neglectedly; numbly; painedly; painfully; painstakingly; palely; pallidly; pathetically; pensively; pessimistically; piteously; pitifully; pleadingly; powerlessly; purposelessly; quaveringly; regretfully; rejectedly; remorsefully; remotely; resignedly; ruefully; saddenedly; sadly; self-critically; self-deprecatingly; self-effacingly; self-pityingly; sentimentally; shakily; shakingly; shamefacedly; shiveringly; sobbingly; solemnly; somberly; sorely; sorrowfully; soulfully; sourly; spiritlessly; strainedly; strainingly; strangledly; stressedly; stressfully; sufferingly; sulkily; sullenly; tearfully; tearily; temperamentally; thinly; tonelessly; tormentedly; tornly; torturously; touchily; tragically; traumatically; tremblingly; tremulously; troubledly; tumultuously; tunelessly; turbulently; uncheerfully; unconsolably; uncontrollably; unevenly; unhappily; unharmoniously; unmotivatedly; unreservedly; unrestrainedly; unsettledly; unsmilingly; unsteadily; upsetly; vacantly; vulnerably; waifishly; wanly; waveringly; weakly; wearily; wearisomely; weepily; whinily; whiningly; wintrily; wispily; witheringly; woefully; woundedly; wretchedly.

USAGE EXAMPLES

"Please, don't leave," she said *anguishedly*.

"Tell me," he asked *defeatedly*, "what's the point of trying?"

"I can't seem to ever get it right," Don said *hollowly*.

"You can do whatever you want," she muttered *miserably*. "Meanwhile, I'm stuck here."

"I won't let you treat me like this!" Carol shouted *tearfully*.

Emotion: Surprise

aghastly; alarmedly; alarmingly; alertly; amazedly; astonishedly; astoundedly; awedly; awesomely; awestruckly; baffledly; bafflingly; befuddledly; bewilderedly; bewilderingly; faintheartedly; flabbergastedly; flummoxedly; frenziedly; galvanically; galvanizingly; gaspingly; hair-raisingly; horrifiedly; horrifyingly; hysterically; incredibly; incredulously; jumpily; mystifiedly; outragedly; outrageously; overwhelmedly; overwhelmingly; puzzledly; queryingly; questioningly; quizzically; shakenly; shakily; shakingly; shiveringly; shockedly; shockingly; shrilly; shrinkingly; spellbound; stammeringly; startledly; startlingly; stumblingly; stunnedly; stupefiedly; stutteringly; surprisedly; surprisingly; tremblingly; tremulously; twitchily; twitchingly; unevenly; unexpectedly; wonderingly.

USAGE EXAMPLES

"What are you doing here?" she said *alarmedly*.

"How can you not be upset?" Frank asked *baffledly*.

Outragedly, she said, "Well, I never expected you would double cross me!"

"Yes, of course I'm here alone," the old man said *startledly*.

"Are you sure?" Nicole croaked *stupefiedly*.

Emotion: Unfeeling

aloofly; amorally; apathetically; barefacedly; blandly; blankly; bluntly; boldly; boredly; brazenly; brusquely; calculatingly; candidly; carelessly; casually; cheerlessly; clinically; cold-bloodedly; coldheartedly; coldly; colorlessly; composedly; conservatively; coolly; critically; cuttingly; cynically; dauntlessly; deadpan; detachedly; directly; disconnectedly; disinterestedly; dismissively; dispassionately; distantly; dryly/drily; emotionlessly; emptily; evenly; expressionlessly; firmly; flatly; forthrightly; forwardly; frankly; freezingly; frigidly; frostily; frozenly; glassily; groundedly; hardheartedly; hardly; heartlessly; hollowly; humorlessly; icily; impersonally; imperturbably; indifferently; ingenuously; inhumanely; inhumanly; insensitively; insincerely; insouciantly; leadenly; lifelessly; matter-of-factly; mechanically; mirthlessly; neglectfully; neutrally; nonchalantly; noncommittally; nonjudgmentally; passionlessly; passively; pessimistically; pointblank; resignedly; shamelessly; soberly; solidly; stably; staidly; steadfastly; steadily; stoically; stolidly; stonily; straightfacedly; tactlessly; unaffectedly; unapologetically; unblinkingly; uncaringly; unemotionally; unfeelingly; unsmilingly; vacantly; wolfishly; woodenly.

USAGE EXAMPLES

"I don't care what you do," Kevin said *aloofly*.

"You have a month to live at best," the doctor said *clinically*.

"Take your stuff and get out," his mother said *emotionlessly*.

"Peter has no one to blame but himself," she said *icily*.

"Yes," he answered *soberly*, "I killed him."

Dynamics: Loud

aloud; billowingly; blusteringly; boisterously; boomingly; brassily; cacophonously; chantingly; cheeringly; clamorously; deafeningly; discordantly; ear-piercingly; ear-splittingly; echoingly; enormously; gigantically; gratingly; harshly; hugely; jarringly; loudly; massively;

mightily; noisily; piercingly; plangently; powerfully; raucously; resonantly; reverberantly; ringingly; roaringly; rumblingly; screechingly; shrilly; sonorously; squawkingly; strepitously; stridently; thunderingly; thunderously; tumultuously; turbulently; uproariously; vocally; vociferously.

USAGE EXAMPLES

"Hip, hip, hooray!" her parents sang *boisterously*.

"Let go of me!" she cried *deafeningly* into his ear.

"Get your hands off her!" he said *mightily*.

"Ah, a cockroach!" she cried *shrilly*.

"We're through!" he said *thunderously*.

Dynamics: Soft

airily; breathily; breathlessly; brittlely; damply; diminutively; faintly; fragilely; frailly; gaspingly; gently; hissingly; hushedly; inaudibly; inhalingly; laboredly; lightly; lowly; mentally; mousily; muffledly; mumblingly; murmuringly; mutedly; mutely; mutteringly; noiselessly; nonverbally; quiescently; quietly; reservedly; reticently; secretively; sighingly; softly; squeakily; subduedly; thinly; voicelessly; weakly; whisperingly; wispily; wordlessly.

USAGE EXAMPLES

"Thank you," she said *breathily*, taking his hand.

He spoke *faintly*, "Are you alright, miss?"

"I have a secret," Kelly whispered *lightly* into his ear.

"Yes," Mark agreed *mutedly*.

"Not here!" she objected *softly*.

Sound: Tone

airily; brassily; breathily; brittlely; coarsely; coughingly; creakily; creamily; crescendingly; crisply; croakily; croakingly; deeply; drawlingly; dulcetly; euphoniously; fragilely; frailly; gratingly; grindingly; grittily; groaningly; groggily; growlingly; gruffly; gruntingly; gurglingly; gutturally; harmonically; harshly; hoarsely; huffily; huskily; jaggedly; lispily; lispingly; mellifluously; melodically; melodiously; metallically; monotonously; musically; nasally; raspily; raspingly; resonantly; reverberantly; roughly; rustily; scratchily; shrilly; sibilantly; singingly; squeakily; thickly; thinly; throatily; tonelessly; tunefully; tunelessly.

USAGE EXAMPLES

"Kevin, clean that damn room!" said his mother *brassily*.

"No one can help me," she said *croakily*.

"I have a cold," he said *hoarsely*.

The voice replied *metallically*, "Enter if you dare."

"Oh, alright," Susan acknowledged *raspily*.

Physical State: Hungry / Thirsty

aridly; avidly; breathlessly; carnivorously; cravingly; deprivedly; eagerly; edaciously; emptily; esuriently; faintly; famishedly; gluttonously; greedily; hoggishly; hollowly; hungrily; keenly; lightheadedly; peakily; piggishly; rapaciously; raspily; raspingly; ravenously; sighingly; slobberingly; slothfully; starvingly; thirstily.

USAGE EXAMPLES

Eagerly, she asked, "What's for lunch?"

"Thanks," he said *famishedly*. "I'm starving."

"Bring me more!" the King demanded, *greedily*.

"What time," he asked *hungrily*, "is supper?"

"Fetch me a beer, woman!" Mr. Snow shouted *thirstily*.

Physical State: Sick

achingly; colorlessly; debilitatedly; dizzily; drunkenly; feebly; feverishly; flushedly; gingerly; hazily; hoarsely; inebriatedly; intoxicatedly; lifelessly; limply; nauseatingly; nauseously; painedly; painfully; painstakingly; palely; pallidly; perspiringly; pestiferously; queasily; raspily; raspingly; roughly; scratchily; shakily; shakingly; shiveringly; shudderingly; sickly; sighingly; simperingly; sluggishly; slurringly; sorely; squeamishly; strainingly; strangledly; strenuously; stressedly; sufferingly; tearily; thinly; throatily; tinglingly; tipsily; tonelessly; tormentedly; traumatically; tremblingly; tremulously; waifishly; wanly; weakly; wheezingly; wincingly; woozily.

USAGE EXAMPLES

"I think I'm going to be sick," Katherine said *dizzily*.

"Phew," George said *gingerly*. "I don't feel so hot."

"Is it just me, or is it hot in here?" she asked *perspiringly*.

"I had too much to drink," the old man said *slurringly*.

"Mommy," Nicholas breathed *wheezingly*, "I feel ill."

Physical State: Tired

absently; absentmindedly; catatonically; comatosely; crabbily; crankily; dizzily; drainedly; drowsily; dully; effetely; effortfully; emptily; exhaustedly; exhaustively; faintly; foggily; frazzledly; groggily; grouchily; grumpily; haggardly; irritatedly; lethargically; listlessly;

moodily; pantingly; perspiringly; raggedly; sedately; serenely; sleepily; sluggishly; soporifically; tiredly; tiresomely; tiringly; tranquilly; transfixedly; wearily; wearisomely; windedly; yawningly.

USAGE EXAMPLES

"Dear, come back to bed," she said *drowsily*.

"I'm beat," he breathed *exhaustedly*.

"Sorry I'm late," she said *listlessly* to her boss.

"Just ten more minutes," Alex said *sleepily*.

"What do you want?" he asked *tiredly*.

Manner: Bored

absently; aimlessly; aloofly; apathetically; blandly; blindly; boredly; boringly; catatonically; cheerlessly; despondently; detachedly; disconnectedly; disinterestedly; distantly; distractedly; dully; feebly; flatly; halfheartedly; idly; immovably; indifferently; joylessly; lackadaisically; lacklusterly; lethargically; limply; listlessly; mellowly; monotonously; mopingly; mundanely; nonchalantly; nonplussedly; numbly; passively; perfunctorily; remotely; resignedly; restlessly; routinely; sedatedly; sedately; slackly; sourily; spiritlessly; stuporously; subduedly; trailingly; unambitiously; unconcernedly; unenthusiastically; unexcitedly; unfocusedly; uninquisitively; uninspiredly; uninterestedly; unmotivatedly; unmovingly; unproductively; unresponsively; vacantly; weakly; wearily; yawningly.

USAGE EXAMPLES

"No, I don't want to," Peter said *apathetically*.

"The name sounds familiar," she said *boredly*. "I may have been there before."

"I have nothing in common with her anyway," he said *indifferently*.

"No one understands what it's like," she said *remotely*.

Unexcitedly, Cathy asked, "What are they going to do here?"

Manner: Confused

absently; absentmindedly; absurdly; addledly; aimlessly; ambivalently; asininely; baffledly; bafflingly; befuddledly; bewilderedly; bewilderingly; blankly; blindly; capriciously; cluelessly; confusedly; confusingly; daftly; dazedly; deludedly; densely; derangedly; dimly; dimwittedly; discombobulatedly; disconcertedly; disorganizedly; disorientedly; ditzily; dully; dumbfoundedly; dumbly; erratically; fatuously; flummoxedly; foolishly; forgetfully; glibly; groundlessly; hyperbolically; idiotically; ignorantly; illogically; implausibly; inaccurately; inanely; inaptly; incoherently; incompetently; incomprehendingly; incomprehensibly; inconclusively; incorrectly; ineptly; inexactly; irrationally; ludicrously; meanderingly; meaninglessly; mindlessly; misguidedly; misguidingly; mistakenly; moronically; morosely; muddledly; mystifiedly; nonsensically; obliviously; obtusely; perplexedly; pointlessly; preposterously; puzzledly; ramblingly; randomly; rantingly; reasonlessly; repetitiously; ridiculously; stumpedly; stupidly; thickheadedly; transfixedly; uncleverly; uncomprehendingly; uncritically; unenlightenedly; uninformatively; unintelligently; unknowingly; unquestioningly; unsurely; unwisely; uselessly; vacuously; witlessly.

USAGE EXAMPLES

"Those men can live on sunlight, you know," she said *absentmindedly*.

"Uh, yeah," Ben replied *befuddledly*. "I think so."

"The house was right here," she exclaimed *confusedly*.

"Now, where did I put my car keys?" Lucy said *forgetfully*.

"What?" Markus said *puzzledly*. "What is he talking about, Andrew?"

Manner: Critical

admonishingly; adversarially; analytically; appraisingly; approvingly; argumentatively; assessingly; belittlingly; biasedly; bitingly; captiously; cavillously; censoriously; challengingly; condemningly; condescendingly; correctively; critically; cuttingly; cynically; damningly; demandingly; demeaningly; denouncingly; deploringly; deprecatingly; deprecatively; derogatorily; disapprovingly; disbelievingly; discernibly; discerningly; discriminatingly; disfavorably; dismissingly; dismissively; disparagingly; doubtfully; doubtingly; evaluatingly; exactingly; exceptively; fastidiously; ficklely; finickily; finickingly; floutingly; fussily; impartially; intolerantly; judgmentally; judiciously; knowingly; naggingly; narrow-mindedly; nigglingly; nit-pickingly; objectively; opinionatedly; opposingly; overcritically; patronizingly; pejoratively; pessimistically; pickily; prejudgementally; prejudicedly; priggishly; pushily; rebukingly; remonstrantly; remonstratively; reprimandingly; reproachfully; reprovingly; sardonically; scoldingly; self-critically; self-deprecatingly; self-effacingly; self-mockingly; severely; sharply; skeptically; slanderously; trenchantly; unbelievingly; unbiasedly; unconvincedly; witheringly.

USAGE EXAMPLES

"Samantha," her father said *admonishingly*. "Be nice to your cousin."

"So," he said *assessingly*, "I see you only scored a 94 on your entrance exam."

"Stop slouching, Amanda!" Madam Bromell hissed *critically*.

Judgmentally, he said, "You know, your son is a bad egg."

"Keep silent, Susan," Mrs. Connors lisped *reproachfully*.

Manner: Deceptive

beguilingly; believably; cagily; calculatingly; clandestinely; coaxingly; confidentially; conflictedly; connivingly; conspiratorially; contrivedly; controlledly; convincingly; covertly; cunningly; deceitfully; deceptively;

denyingly; deviously; dishonestly; disingenuously; distrustfully; distrustingly; dubiously; evasively; facetiously; fallaciously; falsely; farcically; feignedly; fibbingly; fraudulently; furtively; guilefully; guiltily; imitatively; incongrously; manipulatively; mischievously; misleadingly; mistrustfully; mistrustingly; opportunistically; ostensibly; paradoxically; perfidiously; persuasively; pliantly; predatorily; ruthlessly; sarcastically; satirically; schemingly; secretively; shiftily; shiftingly; shrewdly; sinfully; sinisterly; sketchily; sleekly; slickly; slyly; smoothly; sneakily; stealthily; straightfacedly; subversively; surreptitiously; suspectingly; suspiciously; tactically; traitorously; treacherously; treasonably; treasonously; trickily; twistedly; twitchily; twitchingly; underhandedly; unevenly; unreliably; unscrupulously; untruthfully; unvirtuously; wilily; wolfishly.

USAGE EXAMPLES

"Depends," Dennis said *cagily*. "What are you offering?"

"I miss her a lot," he said *contrivedly*.

"Well, I'll see you later," she said *evasively*.

"Tell me, is Mr. Jones married?" Karen asked *schemingly*.

Shiftily, he asked, "Do you mind if I use the bathroom?"

Manner: Disgusted

abhorrently; crudely; despicably; detestably; disgustedly; disgustingly; execrably; fetidly; filthily; foully; foulmouthedly; freakishly; fulsomely; grossly; grotesquely; gruesomely; immorally; indecently; indecorously; lewdly; licentiously; loathsomely; malodorously; nauseatingly; noxiously; obscenely; offensively; perversely; pervertedly; poisonously; putridly; rancidly; repulsedly; repulsively; revoltingly; salaciously; shamelessly; shockingly; sickeningly; slimily; sordidly; tastelessly; vilely; vulgarly; wickedly.

USAGE EXAMPLES

"She won't get a boyfriend if she doesn't put out," Wendy said *crudely*.

"We all like the taste of blood," Victor hissed *foully*.

"No one cares when you're dead," he said *indecently*.

"It is only one night," the old man whispered *perversely*.

Slimily, the boy approached the girls and asked, "Which one of youse is gonna be my bitch?"

Manner: Embarrassed

abashedly; apprehensively; awkwardly; bashfully; clammily; disconcertedly; disconcertingly; embarrassedly; floridly; flusteredly; humiliatedly; humiliatingly; mortifiedly; nervously; red-facedly; reddeningly; self-consciously; shamefacedly; shamefully; sheepishly; shrinkingly; shyly; skittishly; squeamishly; stammeringly; stunnedly; stutteringly; surprisedly; traumatically; tremulously; uncomfortably; unevenly; unnervedly.

USAGE EXAMPLES

"Sorry about that," Lilly said *abashedly*.

"I don't have anymore," he said *clammily*.

"No, you go first," she said *flusteredly*.

Self-consciously, she whimpered, "Can I be excused?"

Trudy uttered *shyly*, "I forgot my lines."

Manner: Jealous

accusatively; accusatorily; accusingly; adversarially; anxiously; argumentatively; avariciously; begrudgingly; bitchily; bitterly; brattily; broodingly; callously; callowly; cattily; childishly; competitively;

confrontationally; connivingly; contemptibly; contemptuously; covetously; cunningly; cuttingly; demandingly; doubtingly; dramatically; embitteredly; emotionally; enviably; enviously; greedily; grudgingly; guardedly; immaturely; insinuatingly; jealously; manipulatively; melodramatically; mistrustfully; paranoidly; paternally; piercingly; possessively; protectively; pryingly; questioningly; resentfully; rottenly; saltily; scandalously; scornedly; scornfully; skeptically; solicitously; stingingly; sulkily; suspectingly; suspiciously; threateningly; unfaithfully; unromantically; untrustingly; vigilantly; warily; watchfully; woundedly; wrathfully; zealously.

USAGE EXAMPLES

"Where were you last night?" she asked *accusatively*.

"I hate the way he looks," he said *bitterly*.

Helen asked *covetously*, "Did your mother leave you anything in her will?"

Enviously, Bridget whispered, "She isn't all that pretty anyway."

"Fine," he said *resentfully*, "leave me here to look after your stupid cats."

Manner: Pandering

abidingly; accessibly; accommodatingly; acknowledgingly; affirmatively; affirmingly; agreeably; agreeingly; amenably; amicably; apologetically; appeasingly; assentingly; complaisantly; compliantly; complicitly; complimentarily; compromisingly; concedingly; confirmingly; congenially; consentingly; convivially; cooperatively; credulously; docilely; flatteringly; friendlily; generously; genially; goodnaturedly; hospitably; idolizingly; ingratiatingly; invitingly; leisurely; loyally; obediently; obligedly; obligingly; obsequiously; panderingly; peaceably; peacefully; permissively; piously; placatingly; positively; profusely; propitiatingly; propitiously; receptively; reciprocatively; salutatorily; selflessly; servilely; sincerely; slavishly; smarmily; submissively; subserviently; suppliantly; supplicatingly; supportively; surrenderingly; sycophantically; trustingly; unimposingly; uxoriously; veneratively; vyingly; worshipfully; worshippingly; yieldingly.

"Can I get you anything else, Sir?" she asked *accommodatingly*.

"Yes, of course," he said *agreeingly*. "The man deserved it."

Docilely, she replied, "Whatever you think is best."

"I will do anything you ask of me," he said *loyally*.

"I aim to please," she whispered *subserviently*.

Manner: Polite

abidingly; acceptingly; accessibly; accommodatingly; acknowledgingly; affably; amiably; banteringly; casually; charmingly; chattily; chivalrously; civilly; classily; complimentarily; considerately; conversationally; cordially; courteously; cultivatedly; culturedly; decently; deferentially; formally; friendlily; genially; genteelly; gentlemanly; good-naturedly; graciously; hospitably; mannerly; mild-manneredly; nicely; obeisantly; obligingly; pleasantly; pleasingly; polishedly; politely; primly; punctiliously; punctually; respectfully; smilingly; smoothly; sociably; thankfully; thoughtfully; unimposingly; warmly; welcomingly; well-manneredly; well-meaningly.

USAGE EXAMPLES

"Good morning," he said *affably* as she entered the room.

"Pleased to meet you," Robert said *charmingly*.

Alfred said *formally*, "The guests have arrived, Sir."

"May I use the restroom?" she asked *politely*.

"I'm glad you could make it," Daniel said *welcomingly*.

Manner: Proud / Austere

accomplishedly; ambitiously; approvingly; aristocratically; arrogantly; assertively; audaciously; auspiciously; austerely; authoritatively; autocratically; autonomously; boastfully; boastingly; boldly; bossily; braggingly; brilliantly; cavalierly; charismatically; charmingly; chauvinistically; cockily; commandingly; complacently; conceitedly; condescendingly; confidently; cultivatedly; culturedly; dapperly; debonairly; decorously; despotically; deviously; dictatorily; dignifiedly; distinguishedly; dominantly; domineeringly; draconially; dutifully; egotistically; elegantly; exaltedly; flamboyantly; foppishly; garishly; gaudily; gloatingly; grandiosely; grandly; haughtily; immodestly; impeccably; imperiously; indulgently; loftily; magisterially; magnanimously; magniloquently; masterfully; momentously; narcissistically; nobly; obnoxiously; oppressively; orderingly; ostentatiously; outspokenly; overconfidently; patriarchally; patriotically; peremptorily; piquantly; platitudinously; poisedly; polishedly; pompously; pontifically; portentously; pretentiously; pridefully; prissily; pristinely; prodigally; proudly; puissantly; refinedly; regally; righteously; royally; sanctimoniously; satisfiedly; savoringly; self-absorbedly; self-approvingly; self-assuredly; self-centeredly; self-confidently; self-importantly; self-interestedly; self-possessedly; self-righteously; self-satisfiedly; sententiously; showily; smugly; snobbily; snobbishly; snootily; sophisticatedly; stylishly; suavely; superciliously; superiorily; swaggeringly; triumphantly; tyrannically; unctuously; urbanely; vaingloriously; vainly; victoriously; wryly.

USAGE EXAMPLES

"Don't speak to me in that tone," she said *aristocratically*.

He *austerely* said: "We have no time for pointless pursuits."

"I demand a room at once," he said *domineeringly*.

Pompously, Andrew broke in, "Well, what do you expect from a savage!"

"Care for a Chardonnay?" the gentleman asked *refinedly*.

Manner: Rude

abrasively; abruptly; abusively; affrontedly; antisocially; backhandedly; bad-manneredly; barbarically; barbarously; bluntly; boorishly; bossily; brusquely; brutishly; bullyingly; caddishly; cantankerously; carelessly; chauvinistically; classlessly; coarsely; complainingly; contumeliously; crassly; crudely; curtly; defamatorily; demandingly; deplorably; derogatively; discordantly; discourteously; disobligingly; disrespectfully; disruptively; distastefully; flagrantly; flippantly; gracelessly; impertinently; impolitely; imprudently; impudently; impulsively; inappropriately; inconsiderately; indecently; indecorously; indelicately; indignantly; inharmoniously; inimically; insensitively; insincerely; insolently; insubordinately; insultingly; lewdly; libelously; loutishly; negatively; obscenely; offhandedly; pesteringly; rashly; rudely; snidely; tactlessly; tartly; tastelessly; thanklessly; thoughtlessly; unamiably; unapologetically; unceremoniously; uncharitably; uncivilly; uncommunicatively; uncordially; uncouthly; unethically; ungenerously; ungenially; ungraciously; ungratefully; unharmoniously; uninhibitedly; unkindly; unpleasantly; unprofessionally; unrefinedly; unwelcomingly.

USAGE EXAMPLES

"I don't care what you think," Martin said *abrasively*.

"No," he said *bluntly*. "I don't need your help."

"Hey you," she demanded *impolitely*, "get me a drink."

Thanklessly, she replied: "Now fetch me my coat."

"Perhaps if you weren't so thick," he said *unkindly*, "you wouldn't need a handout."

Manner: Serious / Rational

academically; accurately; adroitly; amorally; analytically; aptly; articulately; astutely; bluffly; bluntly; briefly; briskly; candidly; civilly; clinically; cogently; competently; composedly; concisely; conscientiously; consideringly; critically; darkly; deadpan; decisively;

deductively; diligently; diplomatically; directly; direly; dryly/drily; educationally; eloquently; enlightenedly; enquiringly; enterprisingly; eruditely; expansively; experiencedly; expertly; explanatively; explicitly; factually; fairly; firmly; flatly; fluently; formally; forthrightly; forwardly; frankly; frugally; geekily; groundedly; heavily; heedfully; helpfully; illuminatedly; illustratively; importantly; informatively; ingeniously; instructively; intelligently; intensely; intently; interrogatively; knowledgeably; laboriously; laconically; learnedly; legalistically; lengthily; leniently; limpidly; logically; long-windedly; matter-of-factly; maturely; meaningfully; measuredly; meditatively; methodically; meticulously; militaristically; mindfully; morally; notably; observantly; officially; passionlessly; patiently; pedantically; penetratingly; perspicaciously; perspicuously; pertinently; philosophically; plainly; poignantly; pointblank; pointedly; politically; potently; powerfully; practically; pragmatically; precisely; probingly; professionally; proficiently; progressively; prolifically; prosaically; prosily; puritanically; purposefully; rationally; realistically; realizingly; reasonably; responsibly; restrainedly; rhetorically; rigidly; sagaciously; sagely; scholastically; scientifically; sensibly; seriously; severely; sharply; shrewdly; significantly; simply; skillfully; smartly; soberly; staunchly; steadfastly; steelily; sternly; stiffly; stoically; stolidly; stonily; straightfacedly; strategically; strictly; studiously; systematically; tautly; tensely; tersely; theoretically; tightly; unamusedly; unblinkingly; unerringly; unfalteringly; unfazedly; unflinchingly; unsmilingly; validly; verbosely; warningly; weightily; wisely; wordily.

USAGE EXAMPLES

"According to statistics," he said *academically*, "most people are unable to cope with stress."

"I tried to do my part," she said *conscientiously*. "Unfortunately, they didn't let me."

"The seas of change are upon us," the CEO said *eloquently*.

David replied *matter-of-factly*, "Perhaps you should concentrate on your own job."

"Children need love to flourish," she offered *sagely*.

Manner: Stubborn

adamantly; anarchically; antagonistically; antisocially; argumentatively; bossily; brattily; bullheadedly; cantankerously; close-mindedly; combatively; contumaciously; defiantly; determinedly; disagreeably; disagreeingly; disobediently; dissentingly; doggedly; dogmatically; formidably; hardheadedly; immovably; immutably; impedingly; impertinently; implacably; inflexibly; intransigently; mulishly; mutinously; noncompliantly; obdurately; obstinately; obstreperously; obtrusively; offensively; opinionatedly; opposedly; perseveringly; persistently; pertinaciously; petulantly; pigheadedly; protestingly; rebelliously; recalcitrantly; refractorily; resolutely; resolvedly; rigidly; singlemindedly; stubbornly; territorially; unbendingly; uncompliantly; uncompromisingly; uncooperatively; unequivocally; unreasonably; unreceptively; unrelentingly; unshakably; unwaveringly; unwillingly; unyieldingly; willfully.

USAGE EXAMPLES

"I'd like to see you try and make me," Gavin said *antagonistically*.

She said *combatively*, "No one is going to stop me!"

"Sorry, but I refuse," he said *inflexibly*.

"Mom, can I have an ice cream?" Nick continued *persistently*.

"Stay off my damn lawn," the old man yelled *territorially*.

Manner: Truthful

believably; candidly; conspicuously; correctly; factually; faithfully; forthrightly; frankly; genuinely; guilelessly; honestly; ingenuously; innocently; justifiedly; justly; kosherly; legitimately; naturally; openly; outrightly; outspokenly; pellucidly; plainly; plausibly; precisely; realistically; reliably; righteously; scrupulously; simply; sincerely; squarely; straightforwardly; trustingly; trustworthily; truthfully; unaffectedly; unfeignedly; unreservedly; unstudiedly; veraciously; verbatim; veritably; vindicatedly; virtuously.

USAGE EXAMPLES

"I don't deny it," Vivian said *candidly*.

"She can't cook worth a damn," her father said *frankly*.

Openly, she spoke for the first time. "I can tell you only what I know."

He said *sincerely*, "I will do what I can to help you."

"Jake was the one who started the fire," Michael responded *truthfully*.

Manner: Vague

abstractly; abstrusely; allegorically; alliteratively; alludingly; allusively; ambiguously; arbitrarily; arcanely; bewilderingly; bizarrely; cryptically; elusively; enigmatically; esoterically; euphemistically; exotically; figuratively; foreignly; hiddenly; idiosyncratically; implicitly; indirectly; indistinctly; metaphorically; mysteriously; mystically; obliquely; obscurely; partially; peculiarly; poetically; queerly; strangely; symbolically; unclearly; undecipherably; unintelligibly; vaguely; weirdly.

USAGE EXAMPLES

"Judgments of the sky," she said *abstractly*.

"Well," Ollie said *ambiguously*, "she's a lot of things."

"I know all," the man said *cryptically*.

"Hath ye no Gods?" he replied *mysteriously*.

"We come, we go, we flow," Mr. Andrews said *vaguely*.

3

Feelings, Emotions, and Internal Dialogue

Emotion and *feeling* **words are used to express a character's emotional state.** *Internal dialogue* **and** *thought tags* **are used when you want to reveal a character's inner thoughts.**

Feelings and Emotions in Alphabetical Order

A – Adjectives

abandoned; abashed; abhorred; abhorrent; abnormal; abominable; abrasive; absent-minded; absolved; absorbed; absurd; abused; abusive; abysmal; accepted; accepting; accessible; acclimated; accommodating; accomplished; accountable; accusatory; accused; acrimonious; adamant; addled; adequate; admirable; admiring; admonished; adorable; adoring; adrift; adventurous; adversarial; affable; affected; affectionate; afflicted; affronted; afraid; aggravated; aggressive; aggrieved; aghast; agitated; agog; agonized; agreeable; aimless; alarmed; alert; alienated; alive; alluring; allusive; almighty; alone; aloof; altruistic; amazed; ambitious; ambivalent; amenable; amoral; amorous; amused; anarchic; angelic; angerless; angry; angsty; anguished; animalistic; animated; annoyed; antagonistic; anticipatory; antipathetic; antisocial; antsy; anxious; apathetic; apologetic; appalled; appreciated; appreciative; apprehensive; ardent; argumentative; aristocratic; aroused; arrogant; ashamed; asinine; asleep; assertive; assured; astonished; astounded; astute; atrocious; attached; attacked; attentive; attracted; attractive; audacious; august; auspicious; austere; authoritative; autocratic; autonomous; avaricious; aversive; avid; awake; aware; awed; awesome; awestruck; awful; awkward.

A – Nouns / Phrases

abandonment; abashedness; abrasiveness; absolution; absurdity; abuse; acceptance; accessibility; accommodation; adamant; admirability;

admiration; admonishment; adorability; adoration; adventurousness; affability; affection; aggravation; aggression / aggressiveness; aggrievement; agitation; agony; agreement; aimlessness; alert / alertness; alienation; allure; allusiveness; aloneness; altruism; amazement; ambition / ambitiousness; ambivalence; amorality; amorousness / amorosity; amusement; anarchy; anger; angerlessness; angst; anguish; animation; animosity; annoyance; antagonism; anticipation; antipathy; antsiness; anxiety; apathy; appreciation; apprehension; ardency; arousal; arrogance; assertiveness; astonishment; astoundment; astuteness; at a loss; at ease; at home; at peace; attentiveness; attraction; at war with (...); audaciousness / audacity; augustness; auspiciousness; austereness; autonomy; avarice; aversion; avidness; awe; awkwardness.

B – Adjectives

babied; bad; bad-tempered; badgered; baffled; baited; balanced; ballistic; bamboozled; banal; barren; bashful; battered; batty; bawdy; bearable; bearish; beastly; beat; beaten; beaten down; beautiful; bedazzled; bedeviled; befuddled; begrudged; beguiled; beholden; beleaguered; belittled; bellicose; belligerent; belonging; beloved; below average; bemused; benevolent; benign; berated; bereaved; bereft; berserk; beseeched; beset; besieged; besmirched; besotted; bested; bestial; betrayed; better; bewildered; bewitched; biased; big; bilious; bitched at; bitchy; bitter; bittersweet; bizarre; blamed; blameless; bland; blank; blanketed; blasphemous; blasé; bleak; bled dry; blessed; blighted; blind; blissful; blithe; bloated; bloodthirsty; blown away; bludgeoned; blue; blurry; blustered; boastful; bodacious; boggled; bogus; boisterous; bold; bombarded; bombastic; boorish; bored; bossed around; bossy; bothered; bothersome; bottled up; bought; bouncy; bound; bounded; boundless; bowled over; boxed in; boxed out; brainless; brainwashed; brainy; brash; bratty; brave; brazen; breathless; breathtaken; breezy; bridled; bright; bright eyed; brilliant; brisk; bristling; broad-minded; broken; broken down; brokenhearted; broken up; broody; browbeaten; bruised; brushed off; brutalized; brutish; bubbly; bugged; buggered; bulldozed; bullied; bullish; bummed; bummed out; buoyant; burdened; burdensome; burly; burned; burned out; burned up; bursting; buzzed.

B – Nouns / Phrases

babyishness; badness; bafflement; bamboozlement; banality; barrenness; bashfulness; battiness; bawdiness; bearishness; beastliness; beauty; bedazzlement; befuddlement; beguilement; belittlement; bellicosity; belligerence; belongingness; bemusement; benevolence; benignity; bent out of shape; bereavement; berserkness; beseechingness; besetment; besiegement; besottedness; bestiality; betrayal; betterment; bewilderment; bewitchment; bias; bigness; biliousness; bitchiness; bitterness; bittersweetness; bizarreness; blamelessness; blandness; blanketedness; blankness; blasphemy; bleakness; blessedness; blight; blindness; bliss; blitheness; bloatedness; bloodthirstiness; blueness; blurriness; boastfulness; bogusness; boisterousness; boldness; boorishness; boredom; bossiness; bounciness; boundedness; boundlessness; braininess; brainlessness; brashness; brattiness; bravery; brazenness; breathlessness; breeziness; brightness; brilliance; broad-mindedness; brokenheartedness; brokenness; broodiness; brutality; brutishness; bullishness; buoyancy; burliness.

C – Adjectives

caged; caged in; cagey; cajoled; calculating; callous; callow; calm; canny; cantankerous; capable; capricious; captious; captivated; captive; captured; cared for; carefree; careful; careless; careworn; caring; carried away; castigated; cast out; catatonic; cathartic; catty; caught out; cautious; cavalier; censored; censured; centered; certain; chafed; chagrined; chained; challenged; changed; chaotic; charged; charismatic; charitable; charmed; charming; chased; chaste; chastised; chatty; cheap; cheapened; cheated; cheated on; cheeky; cheerful; cheerless; cheery; cherished; chic; chicken; chided; childish; childlike; chilled; chilly; chipper; chivalrous; choked up; choosy; chosen; chuffed; churlish; circumspect; circumvented; civil; civilized; clammy; classy; claustrophobic; clean; cleansed; clear; clear-headed; clever; clingy; cloistered; closed; closed-minded; closed off; clouded; clued in; clueless; clumsy; coarse; coaxed; cocky; coddled; codependent; coerced; cold; cold-blooded; cold-hearted; collected; colorful; colossal; comatose; combative; comfortable; comforted; comfy; commanding; committed; common; communicative; compassionate; compatible; compelled; competent; competitive; complacent; complete; complex; compliant; complicated; composed; compromised; compulsive; conceited; concentrated; concerned; condemned; condescended to; condescending; confident; confined; conflicted; confounded; confronted; confronting; confused; connected; conned; conniving; conquered; conscientious; conscious; conservative; considerate; consoled; consoling; conspicuous; conspiratorial; conspired against; constrained; constricted; constructive; consumed; contagious; contained; contaminated; contemplative; contemptible; contemptuous; content; contented; contentious; contrite; controlled; controlling; convinced; convivial; cool; cooped up;

cooperative; copacetic; cordial; cornered; corralled; correct; corrupted; courageous; courteous; courtly; coveted; covetous; cowardly; coy; cozy; crabby; crafty; cramped; cranky; crappy; crass; craven; crazed; crazy; creative; credulous; creeped out; creepy; crestfallen; criminal; crippled; critical; criticized; cross; crotchety; crowded; crucified; crude; cruel; crummy; crushed; cuckolded; cuckoo; cuddly; culpable; cultured; cumbersome; cunning; curious; curmudgeonly; cursed; cut; cut down; cut off; cute; cynical.

C – Nouns / Phrases

caginess; callousness; callowness; calmness; canniness; cantankerousness; capability; caprice / capriciousness; captiousness; captivation; care; carefulness; carelessness; castigation; catharsis; cattiness; caution / cautiousness; cavalierism / cavalierness; centeredness; certainty; chagrin; challenge; change; chaos; charisma; charity; charm; chastisement; chastity / chasteness; chattiness; cheapness; cheekiness; cheerfulness; cheeriness; cheerlessness; childishness; chilliness; chivalry; choosiness; churlishness; circumspection; circumvention; civility; clamminess; clarity; classiness; claustrophobia; cleanliness; clear-headedness; cleverness; clinginess; cloistered; closed-mindedness; close to (...); closure; cluelessness; clumsiness; coarseness; cockiness; codependency; coercion; cold-bloodedness; cold-heartedness; coldness; colossality; combativeness; comfiness; comfort; comfortability; command; commitment; commonality; compassion; compatibility; competence; competition; complacency; completeness; complexity; compliance; composure; compromise; compulsion; conceit; concentration; concern; condemnation; condescension; confidence; confinement; conflict; confrontation; confusion; connection; conscientiousness; consciousness; conservativeness; consideration; conspicuousness; constraint; constriction; constructiveness; consumption; contagiousness; contamination; contemplation; contempt; contemptibility; contentedness; contentiousness; contrary to (...); contrition; control; conviviality; coolness; cooperation; cordiality / cordialness; correctness; corruption; courage / courageousness; courtesy / courteousness; courtliness; covetousness; cowardliness; coyness; coziness; crabbiness; craftiness; crankiness; crappiness; crassness; cravenness; craziness; creativeness; credulity / credulousness; creepiness; criminality; criticism; crossness; crotchetiness; crudeness; cruelty; crumminess; cuddliness; culpability; culture; cumbersomeness; cunningness; curiosity / curiousness; cuteness; cynicalness.

D – *Adjectives*

daffy; dainty; damaged; damned; dandy; dangerous; dapper; daring; dark; dashed; dashing; dastardly; daunted; dauntless; dazed; dazzled; dazzling; dead; deafened; debased; debauched; debilitated; debonair; decadent; deceitful; deceived; decent; deceptive; decided; decimated; decisive; decorous; decrepit; dedicated; deep; defeated; defective; defenseless; defensive; deferential; defiant; deficient; defiled; definite; deflated; deformed; degenerate; degraded; dehumanized; dejected; delicate; delighted; delightful; delinquent; delirious; delivered; deluded; demanding; demeaned; demeaning; demented; democratic; demolished; demonized; demoralized; demotivated; demure; denatured; denigrated; denounced; dense; dependent; depleted; depraved; depressed; deprived; derailed; deranged; derided; derisive; deserted; deserving; desirable; desired; desirous; desolate; despairing; desperate; despicable; despised; despondent; destitute; destroyed; destructive; detached; determined; detestable; detested; devalued; devastated; deviant; devil-may-care; devious; devoted; devout; diabolical; dictatorial; didactic; different; difficult; diffident; diffused; dignified; diligent; dim; dimensionless; diminished; diminutive; diplomatic; dire; direct; directionless; direful; dirty; disabled; disaffected; disagreeable; disappointed; disapproved of; disapproving; disarmed; disbelieved; disbelieving; discarded; disciplined; discombobulated; discomfited; disconcerted; disconnected; disconsolate; discontent; discontented; discounted; discouraged; discouraging; discredited; discreet; discriminated; discriminating; disdainful; disembodied; disempowered; disenchanted; disenfranchised; disfavored; disgraced; disgraceful; disgruntled; disgusted; disgusting; disharmonious; disheartened; disheveled; dishonest; dishonorable; dishonored; disillusioned; disingenuous; disinterested; disjointed; disliked; disloyal; dismal; dismayed; dismembered; dismissed; dismissive; disobedient; disobeyed; disorderly; disorganized; disoriented; disowned; disparaged; dispassionate; dispensable; dispirited; displaced; displeased; disposable; disquieted; disregarded; disrespected; disrespectful; disruptive; dissatisfied; dissed; dissident; distant; distinguished; distorted; distracted; distraught; distressed; distrusted; distrustful; disturbed; ditched; divergent; diverted; divided; dizzy; docile; dogged; dogmatic; doleful; dolorous; domesticated; dominant; dominated; domineered; domineering; done; doomed; dorky; doted on; doting; double-crossed; doubted; doubtful; dour; dowdy; down; downcast; downhearted; downtrodden; draconian; dragged down; drained; dramatic; drawn in; dreaded; dreadful; dreamy; dreary; driven; droll; drunk; dubious; dull; dulled; dumb; dumbfounded; dumbstruck; duped; dutiful; dwarfed; dynamic; dysfunctional; dysphoric; dysthymic.

D – Nouns / Phrases

daffiness; daintiness; damnation; dandiness; danger; dapperness; daringness; darkness; dastardliness; dauntingness; dauntlessness; daze; deadness; deafness; debasement / debasedness; debauchery; debilitation; debonairness; decadence; deceit; decentness; deception; decimation; decisiveness; decorousness; decrepitness; dedication; defeat; defectiveness; defenselessness; defensiveness; deference; defiance; deficiency; defilement; definiteness; definitiveness; definitude; deflatedness; degeneration; degradation; dehumanization; dejectedness / dejection; delicacy; delight; delinquency; delirium; deliverance; delusion; dementia; democracy; demonization; demoralization; demotivation; demureness; denaturation; denigration; denouncement; denseness / density; dependence; depletion; depravity; depression; deprivation; depth / deepness; derailment; derangement; derision; desertion; desirability; desire; desolation; despair; desperation; despicability / despicableness; despisableness; despondency; destitution; destructiveness; detachment; determination; detestability; devaluation; devastation; deviance; deviousness; devoid of (...); devotion; devoutness; diabolicalness; difference; difficulty; diffidence; diffusion; dignity / dignifiedness; diligence; dimensionlessness; diminishment; diminutiveness; dimness; diplomacy; directionlessness; directness; direness; dirtiness; disability; disaffectedness; disagreeableness / disagreeability; disappointment; disbelief; discipline; discombobulation; discomfort; disconcertion / disconcertment; disconnection; disconsolation / disconsolateness; discontent / discontentment; discouragement; discreetness; discrimination; disdain; disembodiment; disempowerment; disenchantment; disenfranchisement; disfavor; disgrace; disgracefulness; disgruntlement; disgust; disgustingness; disharmony; disheartenment; dishevelment; dishonesty; dishonor; disillusionment; disingenuousness; disinterest; disjointedness; dislike; disloyalty; dismalness / dismality; dismay; dismissiveness; disobedience; disorder; disorganization; disorientation; disparagement; dispassion / dispassionateness; dispensability / dispensableness; dispiritedness; displacement; displeasure; disposability / disposableness; disquiet; disregard; disrespect; disrespectfulness; disruptiveness; dissatisfaction; dissidence; dissonance; distantness; distortedness; distraction; distress; distrust; distrustfulness; divergence; divorced from (...); dizziness; docility; doggedness; dogma; dolefulness; dolorousness; domestication; dominance; domination; doom; dorkiness; doubt; doubtfulness; dourness; dowdiness; downheartedness; drama; drawn toward (...); dread; dreadfulness; dreaminess; dreariness; drive; drollness; drunkenness;

dubiousness; dullness; dumbfoundedness; dumbness; duty / dutifulness; dysfunction; dysphoria; dysthymia.

E – Adjectives

eager; earnest; earthy; eased; easy; easy-going; ebullient; eccentric; eclectic; eclipsed; ecstatic; edgy; edified; effective; effeminate; effervescent; effete; efficacious; efficient; effusive; egocentric; egotistical; elated; electric; electrified; elegant; elevated; elite; eloquent; elusive; emancipated; emasculated; embarrassed; embittered; emboldened; eminent; emotional; emotionless; emotive; empathetic; emphatic; empowered; empty; enabled; enamored; enchanted; enchanting; enclosed; encouraged; encouraging; encroached upon; encumbered; endangered; endeared; endearing; endowed; energetic; energized; enervated; enfeebled; engaged; engrossed; engulfed; enhanced; enigmatic; enlightened; enlivened; enmeshed; ennobled; enormous; enraged; enraptured; enriched; enslaved; entangled; enterprising; entertained; entertaining; enthralled; enthusiastic; enticed; enticing; entitled; entombed; entranced; entrapped; entrenched; entrepreneurial; entrusted; enveloped; envied; envious; equable; equal; equanimous; equipped; erratic; esteemed; estranged; ethereal; euphoric; evasive; evil; eviscerated; examined; exasperated; excellent; excitable; excited; excluded; excoriated; exculpated; execrated; exhausted; exhilarated; exiled; exonerated; expectant; expendable; experienced; exploitative; exploited; explosive; exposed; expressive; extraordinary; extravagant; extroverted; exuberant; exultant.

E – Nouns

eagerness; earnestness; earthiness; ease; easiness; ebullience; eccentricity; eclecticism; ecstasy; edginess; edification; effectiveness / effectivity; effeminateness; effervescence; effeteness; efficaciousness; efficiency; effusiveness; egocentricity; egotism; elation; electricity; electrification; elegance; elevation; elitism; eloquence; elusiveness; emancipation; emasculation; embarrassment; embitterment; eminence; emotion; emotionlessness; empathy; empowerment; emptiness; enchantment; encouragment; encroachment; encumbrance / encumberment; endangerment; endearment; endowment; energy; enervation; enfeeblement; engagement; enhancement; enjoyment; enlightenment; enlivenment; enmeshment; ennoblement; ennui; enormousness / enormity; enragement; enrichment; enslavement; entanglement; enterprise; entertainment; enthralment; enthusiasm; enticement; entitlement; entombment; entrancement; entrapment;

entrenchment; entrustment; envelopment; envy / enviousness; equability; equality; equanimity / equanimousness; erraticism; esteem; estrangement; ethereality / etherealness; euphoria; evasiveness; evil / evilness; evisceration; exasperation; excellence; excitement; excoriation; exculpation; execration; exhaustion; exhilaration; exile; exoneration; expectancy; expectation; expendability; experience; exploitation; explosiveness; extraordinariness; extravagance; extroversion; exuberance / exuberancy; exultance / exultancy.

F – Adjectives

fabulous; facetious; faint; fainthearted; fair; faithful; fake; fallacious; fallible; fallow; false; falsely accused; famished; famous; fanatical; fanciful; fancy; fantabulous; fantastic; farcical; fascinated; fashionable; fast; fastidious; fat; fatalistic; fatigued; fatuous; favored; fawned over; fazed; feared; fearful; fearless; feckless; fed up; feeble; feisty; feminine; ferocious; fertile; fervent; festive; fettered; fickle; fidgety; fiendish; fierce; fiery; filthy; fine; finicky; firm; fit; fixated; flabbergasted; flaky; flamboyant; flashy; flat; flattered; flawed; flawless; flexible; flighty; flippant; flirtatious; floored; flummoxed; flush; flustered; flustrated; focused; foggy; followed; fond; foolhardy; foolish; forbearing; forbidden; forced; forceful; foreign; forgetful; forgiven; forgiving; forgotten; forlorn; formidable; forsaken; fortified; fortunate; foul; forward; fractious; fractured; fragile; fragmented; frail; framed; frank; frantic; fraternal; fraudulent; fraught; frazzled; freaked; freaked out; freakish; freaky; free; frenetic; frenzied; fresh; fretful; fried; friendless; friendly; frightened; frigid; frisky; frivolous; frolicsome; froward; frowned upon; frugal; fruitful; frustrated; fulfilled; full; fun; funereal; funky; funloving; funny; furious; furtive; fussy; futile.

F – Nouns / Phrases

fabulousness; facetiousness; faintheartedness; faintness; fairness; faith; fakeness; fallaciousness; fallibility; fallowness; falseness; fame; fanaticism; fancifulness; fancy; fantasticalness / fantasticality; farcicality / farcicalness; fascination; fashionableness / fashionability; fastidiousness; fastness; fatalism; fatigue; fatness; fatuousness; favor; fear; fearfulness; fearlessness; fecklessness; feebleness; feistiness; femininity; ferocity / ferociousness; fertility / fertileness; fervor; festiveness; fickleness; fiendishness; fierceness; fieriness; filth / filthiness; fineness; firmness; fitness; fixation; flakiness; flamboyance / flamboyancy; flashiness; flatness; flattery; flawedness; flawlessness; flexibility; flightiness; flippancy / flippantness; flirtatiousness; flushness;

focus; fogginess; fondness; foolhardiness; foolishness; forbearance; forbiddenness; forcefulness; foreignness; forgetfulness; forgiveness; forlornness; formidability / formidableness; forsakenness; fortitude; fortune; forwardness; foulness; fractiousness; fracturedness; fragility; fragmentation; frailness; frankness; franticness; fraudulence; freakiness; freakishness; freedom; freneticness; frenzy; freshness; fretfulness; friendlessness; friendliness; fright; frigidity; friskiness; frivolity; frowardness; frugality / frugalness; fruitfulness; frustration; fulfillment; fullness; full of energy; full of life; fun; funkiness; funniness; furtiveness; fury / furiousness; fussiness; futility.

G – Adjectives

gabby; gallant; galled; galvanized; game; gamey / gamy; garbled; garrulous; gauche; gaudy; gawky; gay; geeky; generous; genial; gentle; genuine; ghastly; giant; giddy; gifted; gigantic; giggly; gilded; giving; glad; glamorous; gleeful; glib; gloomy; glorious; glowing; glum; gluttonous; gnawing; goaded; gobsmacked; good; good-looking; good-natured; goofy; gorgeous; graceful; gracious; grand; grandiose; grateful; gratified; grave; gray / grey; great; greedy; green; gregarious; grief-stricken; grim; groggy; groovy; gross; grossed out; grotesque; grouchy; grounded; grown up; grudging; gruesome; grumpy; guarded; guilt-free; guilt-tripped; guiltless; guilty; gullible; gushy; gutless; gutsy; gutted; gypped.

G – Nouns

gabbiness; gallantry; galvanization; gameness; garrulousness; gaucheness; gaudiness; gawkiness / gawkishness; gayness; geekiness; generosity / generousness; geniality; gentleness; ghastliness; giantness; giddiness; giftedness; giganticness; gladness; glamor / glamorousness; glee; glibness; gloom / gloominess; glory; glumness; gluttony / gluttonousness; goodness; goofiness; gorgeousness; grace; graciousness; grandiosity; grandness; gratefulness; gratitude; graveness; grayness / greyness; greatness; greed; gregariousness; grief; grimness; grogginess; grooviness; grossness; grotesqueness; grouchiness; groundedness; grudge; gruesomeness; grumpiness; guardedness; guilt; guiltlessness; gullibility; gushiness; gutlessness; gutsiness.

H – Adjectives

hacked off; haggard; haggled; halfhearted; hallowed; hammered; hampered; handicapped; handsome; hapless; happy; happy-go-lucky; harangued; harassed; hard-headed; hard-hearted; hard-pressed; hardened; hardy; harmed; harmless; harmonious; harried; harrowed; hassled; hasty; hated; hateful; haughty; haunted; hazy; headstrong; heady; healed; healthy; heartbroken; heartened; heartful; heartless; heartrending; heartsick; hearty; heavy-hearted; heckled; helped; helpful; helpless; henpecked; herded; heroic; hesitant; hexed; hideous; high; high-spirited; hilarious; hindered; hip; hoaxed; holistic; hollow; homely; homesick; honest; honorable; honored; hoodwinked; hopeful; hopeless; hormonal; horny; horrendous; horrible; horrific; horrified; horror-stricken; hospitable; hostile; hot; hot-headed; hot-tempered; hounded; huge; humane; humble; humbled; humiliated; humored; humorless; humorous; hung over; hungry; hung up; hunted; hurried; hurt; hustled; hyped-up; hyper; hyperactive; hypervigilant; hypnotized; hypocritical; hypomanic; hysterical.

H – Nouns / Phrases

haggardness; halfheartedness; hallowedness; hamperedness; handsomeness; haplessness; happiness; harassment; hard-headedness; hard-heartedness; hard done by; hardenedness; hardiness; harm; harmlessness; harmony; harrowment; hastiness; hate; hatred; haughtiness; haziness; headiness; health / healthiness; heartbrokenness; heartiness; heartlessness; heartsickness; heavy-heartedness; helpfulness; helplessness; heroicity; hesitancy / hesitation; hideousness; high-spiritedness; highness; hilarity; hipness; hollowness; homeliness; homesickness; honesty; honor; hope; hopelessness; horniness; horribleness; horror; hospitality / hospitableness; hostility; hot-headedness; hotness; hugeness; humaneness; humbleness; humiliation; humility; humor; humorlessness; hunger; hurt; hyperactivity; hypervigilance; hysteria.

I – Adjectives

icky; icy; idealistic; idiotic; idle; idolized; ignoble; ignominious; ignorant; ignored; ill; ill-humored; ill-tempered; illicit; illuminated; illustrious; imaginary; imaginative; imbalanced; immaculate; immature; immense; immobile; immobilized; immodest; immoral; immortal; immune; impaired; impartial; impassioned; impassive; impatient; impeccable; impeded; impelled; imperfect; imperiled; imperious;

impermanent; impermeable; impertinent; imperturbable; impervious; impetuous; impious; impish; implacable; impolite; important; imposed upon; imposing; impotent; impoverished; impractical; impressed; imprisoned; impudent; impugned; impulsive; impure; inactive; inadequate; inane; inattentive; incapable; incapacitated; incensed; incoherent; incompetent; incomplete; inconclusive; incongruent; inconsiderate; inconsolable; inconspicuous; inconvenienced; incorrect; incorrigible; incredible; incredulous; inculcated; indebted; indecent; indecisive; indefinite; indemnified; indentured; independent; indescribable; indestructible; indicted; indifferent; indignant; indiscreet; indoctrinated; indolent; indulgent; industrious; inebriated; ineffective; ineffectual; inefficient; inept; inert; inexperienced; inexplicable; infallible; infamous; infantile; infatuated; infected; inferior; infirm; inflexible; influenced; influential; informal; informed; infuriated; ingenious; ingenuous; ingratiated; inhibited; inhospitable; inhumane; injured; innocent; innovative; inquisitive; insane; insatiable; inscrutable; insecure; insensitive; insightful; insignificant; insincere; insipid; insistent; insolent; insouciant; inspired; instinctive; instructive; insufficient; insulted; intelligent; intense; intent; interested; interesting; interfered with; internal; interrelated; interrogated; interrupted; intimate; intimidated; intimidating; intolerant; intoxicated; intrepid; intrigued; introspective; introverted; intruded upon; intrusive; intuitive; inundated; invalidated; inventive; invested; invigorated; invincible; invisible; invited; inviting; involved; invulnerable; irascible; irate; irked; irrational; irrelevant; irreproachable; irresistible; irresolute; irresponsible; irreverent; irritable; irritated; isolated; itchy.

I – Nouns

iciness; ickiness; idealism; idleness; idolization; ignobility / ignobleness; ignominy / ignominiousness; ignorance; illicitness; illness; illumination; illustriousness; imbalance; immaculacy / immaculateness; immaturity; immensity; immobility; immobilization; immodesty; immorality; immortality; immunity; impartiality; impassiveness; impatience; impeccability; impedance; imperfectness; imperilment; imperiousness; impermanence; impermeability; impertinence; imperturbability; imperviousness; impetuousness; impiousness; impishness; implacability / implacableness; impoliteness; importance; imposition; impotence; impoverishment; impracticality; imprisonment; impudence; impugnability; impulsiveness / impulsivity; impurity; inactivity; inanity; inattentiveness; incapability / incapableness; incapacitation; incoherence; incompetence; incompleteness; inconclusiveness; incongruence; inconsiderateness / inconsideration; inconsolability / inconsolableness;

inconspicuousness; inconvenience; incorrectness; incorrigibility; incredibility / incredibleness; incredulity / incredulousness; inculcation; indebtedness; indecency; indecision / indecisiveness; indefiniteness; indemnity; independence; indescribability; indestructibility; indifference; indiscretion; indoctrination; indolence; indulgence; industriousness; inebriation; ineffectiveness; ineffectualness; inefficiency; ineptitude; inertia; inexperience; inexplicability / inexplicableness; infallibility; infamy / infamousness; infantility; infatuation; inferiority; infirmity; inflexibility; influence; informality; infuriation; ingeniousness; ingenuity / ingenuousness; ingratiation; inhibition; inhospitality; inhumanity; innocence; innovation; inquisitiveness; insanity; insatiability; inscrutability; insecurity; insensitivity; insight; insignificance; insincerity; insipidity / insipidness; insistence; insolence; inspiration; intelligence; intensity; intentness; interest; intimacy; intimidation; intolerance; intoxication; intrepidity / intrepidness; intrigue; introspection; introversion; intrusion; intuition; inundation; invalidation; inventiveness; invincibility; invisibility; involvement; invulnerability; irascibility; irateness; irrationality; irrelevance; irreproachability; irresistibility; irresoluteness; irresponsibility; irreverence; irritability; irritation; isolation; itchiness.

J – Adjectives
jaded; jarred; jaundiced; jaunty; jazzed; jazzy; jealous; jeered; jejune; jeopardized; jerked around; jilted; jinxed; jittery; jocular; jolly; jolted; jostled; jovial; joyful; joyless; joyous; jubilant; judged; judgmental; judicious; juiced; jumbled; jumpy; justified; juvenile.

J – Nouns
jaundice; jealousy; jejunity; jeopardy / in jeopardy; jitters; jocularity; jolliness; joviality / jovialness; joy; joyousness; jubilance; judgment; judiciousness; justification.

K – Adjectives
keen; kept; kicked around; kind; kindhearted; kingly; kinky; knackered; knightly; knocked around; knocked (down); knocked out; knotted (up); knowledgeable; kooky.

K – Nouns

keenness; kindheartedness; kindness; kingliness; kinkiness; knightliness; knowledgeability; kookiness.

L – Adjectives

labeled; labored; lackadaisical; lackluster; laconic; laid back; lambasted; lame; languid; larger than life; lascivious; late; laughed at; lavish; lax; lazy; lean; learned; lecherous; lectured to; led astray; leery; left out; let down; lethargic; level-headed; lewd; liable; liberated; licentious; lied about; lied to; lifeless; light; light-hearted; liked; limited; limp; lionhearted; listless; little; lively; livid; loath; loathed; loathing; loathsome; logical; lonely; lonesome; longing; loopy; loose; lopsided; lost; loud; lousy; loutish; loved; loveless; lovelorn; lovely; lovestruck; loving; low; low-spirited; lowly; loyal; lubricious; luckless; lucky; lucid; ludicrous; lugubrious; luminous; lush; lustful; lusty; luxurious.

L – Nouns

laboredness; lackadaisicalness; lameness; languidness; lasciviousness; lateness; lavishness; laxness; laziness; leanness; learnedness; lechery / lecherousness; leeriness; lethargy; level-headedness; lewdness; liability / liableness; liberation; licentiousness lifelessness; light-heartedness; lightness; limitedness; limpness; listlessness; littleness; liveliness; lividity / lividness; loathness; loneliness; lonesomeness; longing; loopiness; looseness; lopsidedness; loss; loudness; lousiness; loutishness; love; lovelessness; loveliness; lovelornness; lovingness; low-spiritedness; lowliness; lowness; loyalty; lubriciousness; lucidity; luck / luckiness; lucklessness; ludicrousness; lugubriosity / lugubriousness; luminosity / luminance; lushness; lust; lustfulness; luxuriousness.

M – Adjectives

macabre; macho; mad; maddened; magical; magnificent; maimed; majestic; maladjusted; malcontent; malevolent; malicious; maligned; malleable; malnourished; managerial; manhandled; maniacal; manic; manipulated; manipulative; manly; marginalized; marked; marvelous; masochistic; massive; masterful; materialistic; maternal; mature; maudlin; meager; mean; measly; medicated; mediocre; meditative; meek; megalomaniacal; melancholic; mellow; melodramatic; menaced; menacing; mended; merciful; merry; mesmerized; messed up; messy; methodical; meticulous; mighty; militant; mindful; mindless; miniscule;

miraculous; mirthful; mirthless; misanthropic; mischievous; miscreant; miserable; miserly; misguided; misinformed; misled; misrepresented; missed; mistreated; mistrusted; mistrustful; misunderstood; misused; mixed up; mocked; modest; molested; mollified; mollycoddled; momentous; monitored; monstrous; moody; mopey; moral; moralistic; morally bankrupt; morbid; mordant; moribund; moronic; morose; mortified; mothered; motherly; motivated; mournful; mouthy; moved; muddied; muddled; mundane; murderous; murky; mushy; musical; mutinous; mysterious; mystical; mystified.

M – Nouns

machismo; madness; magnificence; majesty; maladjustment; malaise; malcontentedness; malevolence; malice / maliciousness; malleability; malnourishment; mania; manipulation; manliness; marginalization; marvellousness; masochism; massiveness; mastery; materialism; maturity; maudlinism / maudlinness; meagerness; meanness; mediocrity; meditativeness; meekness; megalomania; melancholy; mellowness; melodrama; menace; mercy; merriment; mesmerization; messiness; meticulousness / meticulosity; might / mightiness; militancy; mindfulness; mindlessness; miraculousness; mirth; mischief; miscreancy; miserliness; misery; misgivings; misguidedness; missed; mistreatment; mistrust; mistrustfulness; misunderstanding; mockery; modesty; molestation; mollification; momentousness; moodiness; mopeiness; morality; morbidity; mordancy; moribundity; morosity; mortification; motherliness; motivation; mournfulness; mouthiness; mundanity; murderousness; murkiness; mushiness; mutiny; mystery / mysteriousness; mysticality / mysticalness; mystification.

N – Adjectives

nagged; nailed (down); naive; naked; nameless; narcissistic; narrow-minded; nasty; natural; naughty; nauseated; nebulous; necessary; needed; needled; needless; needy; negated; negative; neglected; negligent; neighborly; nerdy; nervous; nervy; nettled; neurotic; neutral; nice; niggardly; nihilistic; nippy; nit-picky; noble; nomadic; nonchalant; noncommittal; nonconforming; nondescript; nonexistent; nonplussed; normal; nostalgic; nosy; noticed; novel; nullified; numb; nurtured; nurturing; nutty.

N – Nouns

naivety; nakedness; namelessness; narcissism; narrow-mindedness; nastiness; naturalness; naughtiness; nausea; nebulousness; necessity; need; neediness; needlessness; negation; negativity; neglect; negligence; neighborliness; nerdiness; nerves; nervousness; neutrality; niceness; niggardliness; nihilism; nippiness; nobleness; non-commitment; nonchalance; nonconformity; nonexistence; normality; nostalgia; nothing; numbness; nuts.

O – Adjectives

obedient; objectified; obligated; obliged; obliging; oblivious; obnoxious; obscene; obsequious; observant; observed; obsessed; obsessive; obsolete; obstinate; obstructed; odd; off; off balance; offended; offensive; officious; okay; old; old-fashioned; omnipotent; open; open-minded; opinionated; opportunistic; opposed; oppositional; oppressed; optimistic; opulent; ordered around; orderly; organized; orgasmic; ornery; ostentatious; ostracized; ousted; outdone; outgoing; outlandish; outnumbered; out of control; out of place; out of touch; outraged; outrageous; outranked; outreasoned; outspoken; overanxious; overbearing; overcome; overestimated; overjoyed; overloaded; overlooked; overpowered; overprotective; oversensitive; overwhelmed; overworked; overwrought; overzealous; owned.

O – Nouns

obedience; objectification; obligation; obliviousness; obnoxiousness; obscenity; obsequiousness; obsession; obsessiveness; obsolescence; obstinateness; obstruction; oddness; offensiveness; officiousness; oldness; omnipotence; openness; open-mindedness; opinionatedness; opposition; oppression; optimism; opulence / opulency; order; organization; orneriness; ostentatiousness; ostracization; outlandishness; outrage; outrageousness; outspokenness; overanxiety / overanxiousness; overbearingness; overestimation; overprotectiveness; oversensitivity / oversensitiveness; overzealousness.

P – Adjectives

pacified; pained; painful; pampered; panicked; panicky; paralyzed; paranoid; parasitic; pardoned; parsimonious; partial; passionate; passionless; passive; paternal; pathetic; patient; patronizing; peaceful; peachy; peckish; peculiar; pedantic; pedestrian; peeved; peevish;

pensive; peppy; perceptive; peremptory; perfect; perfectionistic; perilous; peripheral; perky; perplexed; persecuted; persevering; persistent; persnickety; perspicacious; persuaded; persuasive; pert; perturbed; perverted; pervious; pesky; pessimistic; pestered; petered out; petrified; petty; petulant; philanthropic; phlegmatic; phony; picked on; pierced; pigeon-holed; pious; piqued; pissed; pissed off; piteous; pitied; pitiful; pitiless; placated; placid; plagued; plain; playful; pleasant; pleased; pleasurable; pliable; pliant; poised; poisoned; polite; pompous; poor; poorly; popular; portentous; positive; possessed; possessive; potent; pouty; powerful; powerless; practical; pragmatic; praised; preached to; precarious; precious; precluded; precocious; prejudged; prejudiced; preoccupied; prepared; preposterous; prescient; pressed; pressured; prestigious; presumptuous; pretentious; pretty; preyed upon; prideful; prim; primal; primitive; prissy; pristine; privileged; prized; proactive; probed; prodigious; productive; profane; professional; promiscuous; propagandistic; propagandized; propelled; proper; prophetic; prosaic; prosperous; protected; protective; proud; provincial; provisional; provocative; provoked; prudish; psyched; psychopathic; psychotic; puerile; pugnacious; pulled apart; pummeled; pumped (up); punch drunk; punched; punished; puny; pure; purged; purposeful; pursued; pushy; pusillanimous; put down; put out; puzzled.

P – Nouns / Phrases

pacification; pain; pamperedness; panic; paralysis; paranoia; parasiticalness; parsimony; partiality; passion; passionlessness; passivity / passiveness; patheticness; patience; patronization; peace; peachiness; peckishness; peculiarity; pedanticalness; pedestrianism; peevishness; pensiveness; peppiness; perceptivity / perceptiveness; peremptoriness; perfection; perfectionistic; peril; perkiness; perplexity; persecution; perseverance; persistence; persnicketiness; perspicaciousness; persuasion; pertness; perturbability; perversion; perviousness; peskiness; pessimism; petrification; pettiness; petulance; phlegmaticness; phoniness; piousness; piteousness; pitilessness; pity; placation; placidity / placidness; plainness; playfulness; pleasantness; pleasure; pliability; poise; politeness; pomp; poorness; popularity; portent; positivity; possession; possessiveness; potency; poutiness; power; powerlessness; practicality; pragmaticism; precariousness; preciousness; preclusion; precociousness; prejudice; preoccupation; preparation; preposterousness; prescience; pressure; prestige; presumption; pretension; prettiness; pride; primitiveness / primitivity; primness; prissiness; privilege; privy to (...); proactivity / proactiveness; prodigiousness; productivity; profanity; professionalism; promiscuousness; prone to (...); properness;

propheticality / propheticalness; prosaicness; prosperousness; protection; proudness; provocativeness; prudishness; psychosis; pugnaciousness; puniness; punishment; purity; purpose; pushed to (...); pushiness; puzzlement.

Q – Adjectives

quaint; qualified; qualmish; quarrelsome; quashed; queasy; queer; querulous; questioned; quick; quiescent; quiet; quirky; quivery; quixotic; quizzed; quizzical.

Q – Nouns

quaintness; qualm; quandary; queasiness; queerness; querulousness; quickness; quiescence; quietness; quietude; quirkiness.

R – Adjectives

rad; radiant; radical; rageful; railroaded; raked over; rambunctious; rancid; randy; ransacked; rapacious; raped; rapt; rapturous; rash; rational; rattled; raunchy; ravenous; ravished; ravishing; raw; re-energized; reactionary; reactive; ready; realistic; reasonable; reassured; rebellious; reborn; rebuffed; rebuked; recalcitrant; receptive; recharged; reckless; reclusive; reconciled; recovered; recuperated; red-hot; redeemed; refined; reflective; refractory; refreshed; refueled; regal; regretful; rejected; rejuvenated; relaxed; released; relentless; reliable; reliant; relieved; religious; reluctant; reminiscent; remiss; remorseful; remorseless; remote; removed; renewed; renowned; repatriated; repelled; repentant; replaceable; replaced; replenished; reprehensible; repressed; reprimanded; reproachful; reproved; repugnant; repulsed; repulsive; resented; resentful; reserved; resigned; resilient; resistant; resolute; resolved; resourceful; respected; respectful; responsible; responsive; rested; restless; restrained; restricted; retaliatory; retarded; reticent; revealed; revengeful; revered; reverent; reviled; revitalized; revived; revolted; revolting; revolutionary; rewarded; rich; ridiculed; ridiculous; right; righteous; rigid; rigorous; riled; ripped; ripped off; riveted; robbed; robotic; robust; romantic; rotten; rough; rowdy; rude; rueful; ruffled; ruined; ruled; run down; rushed; ruthful; ruthless.

R – Nouns

radiance; radicalness; rage; rambunctiousness; rancidness / rancidity; randiness; rapacity / rapaciousness; raptness; rapture; rashness;

rationality; raunchiness; ravenousness; rawness; readiness; realism; reasonability; reassurance; rebellion; recalcitrance; receptivity / receptiveness; recklessness; reconciliation; recuperation; redemption; refinement; reflection; refractoriness; regalness; regret; rejection; rejuvenation; relaxation; release; relentlessness; reliability; reliance; relief; religiousness; reluctance; reminiscence; remissness; remorse; remorselessness; remoteness; removal; renewal; renown; repatriation; repentance; replenishment; reprehensibility; repression; reproachfulness; reproval; repugnance; repulsion; repulsiveness; resentfulness; reservation; resignation; resilience; resistance; resolution; resourcefulness; respect; responsibility; responsiveness; rest; restlessness; restraint; restriction; retaliation; retardation; reticence; revelation; revenge; reverence; revilement; revitalization; revival; revolt; revolution; revulsion; reward; richness; ridicule; ridiculousness; righteousness; rightness; rigidity; rigor; roboticness; robustness; romance; rottenness; roughness; rowdiness; rudeness; ruefulness; ruin; ruthfulness; ruthlessness.

S – Adjectives

sabotaged; sacrificial; sacrilegious; sad; sadistic; safe; sagacious; salacious; sanctimonious; sane; sanguinary; sanguine; sapient; sarcastic; sardonic; sassy; sated; satiated; satisfied; saturnine; saucy; savvy; scandalized; scandalous; scapegoated; scared; scarred; scatterbrained; scattered; scheming; scientific; scintillating; scoffed at; scolded; scorned; scornful; screwed; screwed over; screwed up; scrutinized; scurrilous; seared; second-guessed; second-rate; secure; sedate; seditious; seduced; seductive; seized; selective; self-abasing; self-absorbed; self-accepting; self-aggrandizing; self-assured; self-centered; self-confident; self-conscious; self-critical; self-deprecating; self-destructive; self-disciplined; self-effacing; self-forgiving; self-hating; self-indulgent; self-loathing; self-pitying; self-reliant; self-righteous; self-sacrificing; self-satisfied; self-serving; self-understanding; selfish; selfless; senile; sensational; sensible; sensitive; sensual; sensuous; sentenced; sentimental; separated; serendipitous; serene; serious; servile; set; settled; set up; sexy; shadowed; shaken; shaky; shallow; shamed; shameful; sharp; shattered; sheepish; sheltered; shielded; shocked; shortchanged; shrewd; shunned; shut out; shy; sick; sick at heart; sickened; significant; silenced; silent; silly; simple; sincere; sinful; single-minded; singled out; sinister; skanky; skeptical; sketchy; skillful; skittish; slack; slandered; sleazy; sledged; sleepy; slighted; sloppy; sloshed; slothful; slovenly; slow; sluggish; slutty; sly; small; smarmy;

smart; smashed; smitten; smooth; smothered; smug; snarky; sneaky; snobbish; snobby; snoopy; snubbed; sober; sociable; social; sodden; soft; soft-hearted; sold out; solemn; solitary; somber; soothed; sophisticated; sophomoric; sordid; sore; sorrowful; sorry; sour; spastic; special; speechless; spellbound; spent; spineless; spirited; spiritless; spiteful; splendid; splendiferous; spoiled; spontaneous; spooked; sprightly; spry; spunky; squeamish; stable; stalked; startled; starved; static; stepped on; stereotyped; stern; stiff; stifled; stigmatized; stilted; stimulated; stingy; stodgy; stoic; stolid; stomped on; stoned; stonewalled; strained; stranded; strange; strangled; strengthened; stressed; stretched; stricken; strict; strong; strong-willed; struck down; struck dumb; stubborn; stuck; stuck up; studious; stuffed; stumped; stunned; stunning; stupefied; stupendous; stupid; stylish; suave; subdued; subjugated; submissive; subordinate; subservient; subversive; subverted; successful; suckered; suffering; suffocated; suicidal; sulky; sullen; sullied; sunk; sunny; super; superb; supercilious; superficial; superior; superstitious; supported; supportive; suppressed; sure; surly; surpassed; surprised; surreal; susceptible; suspicious; swamped; sweet; swell; swindled; switched on; sycophantic; sympathetic.

S – Nouns

sabotage; sacrifice; sacrilege; sadism; sadness; safety; sagacity / sagaciousness; salaciousness / salacity; sanctimony / sanctimoniousness; sanguinariness; sanguinity / sanguinness; sanity; sapience / sapiency; sarcasm; sardonicism; sassiness; satiation; satisfaction; saturnineness / saturninity; sauciness; savviness; scandal / scandalousness; scintillation; scorn / scornfulness; scrutiny / scrutinization; scurrilousness; seclusion; security; sedation; sedition; seduction; seductiveness; selectiveness; self-abasement; self-acceptance; self-aggrandizement; self-assurance; self-centeredness; self-confidence; self-consciousness; self-deprecation; self-destruction; self-discipline; self-hate; self-indulgence; self-love; self-pity; self-reliance; self-righteousness; self-sacrifice; self-satisfaction; selfishness; selflessness; senility; sensation; sensibility; sensitivity; sensuality; sensuousness / sensuosity; sentimentality; separation; serendipity; serenity; seriousness; servitude; sexiness; shakiness; shallowness; shame; shamefulness; sharpness; sheepishness; shock; shrewdness; shyness; sickness; significance; silence; silliness; simplicity; sincerity; sinfulness; single-mindedness; sinisterness; skankiness; skepticism; sketchiness; skill / skillfulness; skittishness; slackness; sleaziness; sleepiness; sloppiness; slothfulness; sloven; slowness; sluggishness; sluttiness; slyness; smallness; smarminess; smartness; smoothness; smugness; snarkiness; sneakiness; snobbiness; snoopiness;

soberness; sociability / sociableness; soddenness; soft-heartedness; softness; solemnness; solitude; somberness; sophistication; sordidness; soreness; sorrow; sourness; speechlessness; spinelessness; spiritedness; spiritlessness; spite; splendiferousness; splendor; spontaneity / spontaneousness; sprightliness; spryness; spunkiness; squeamishness; stability; starvation; sternness; stiffness; stigmatization; stimulation; stinginess; stodginess; stolidity / stolidness; strain; strangeness; strength; stress; strictness; strongness; stubbornness; studiousness; stupefaction; stupendousness; stupidity / stupidness; style / stylishness; suaveness; subjugation; submission; subordination; subservience; subversion; subversiveness; success; suffocation; suicide; sulkiness; sullenness; sunniness; superciliousness; superficiality; superiority; superstition; support; supportiveness; suppression; sureness; surliness; surprise; surrealism; susceptibility; suspicion; sweetness; sympathy.

T – Adjectives

talkative; tame; tantalized; tantrumy; taunted; tearful; teary-eyed; teased; temperamental; temperate; tempestuous; tempted; tenacious; tender; tense; tentative; tenuous; tepid; terrible; terrific; terrified; territorial; terrorized; terse; testy; tetchy; thankful; thick; thickheaded; thirsty; thoughtful; threatened; threatening; thrilled; thwarted; timid; timorous; tingly; tipsy; tired; tireless; to blame; tolerant; tormented; torn; torpid; touched; touchy; tough; traitorous; tranquil; trapped; treacherous; treasonous; tremulous; triumphant; troubled; trusted; trusting; trustworthy; truthful; tumultuous; turned off; turned on; tyrannical.

T – Nouns / Phrases

talkativeness; tameness; tantalization; tearfulness; temperateness; tempestuousness; tenacity / tenaciousness; tenderness; tensity / tenseness; tentativeness; tenuousness; tepidity / tepidness; terribleness; territoriality; terror; terseness; testiness; tetchiness; thankfulness; thickheadedness; thickness; thirst; thoughtfulness; threat; thrill; timidity / timidness; timorousness; tingle(s); tiredness; tirelessness; tolerance; torment; torpidity / torpidness; touchiness; toughness; traitorousness; tranquility; treachery; treason; tremulousness; triumph; trouble; trust; truth; tumult; tyranny.

U – Adjectives

ugly; unabashed; unaffected; unafraid; unambitious; unamiable; unamused; unashamed; unattractive; unbalanced; unbelieving; uncared for; uncaring; uncertain; uncheerful; uncomfortable; uncommunicative; uncontrollable; unconvinced; uncouth; undaunted; underestimated; understanding; understood; undeserving; undignified; uneasy; unemotional; unenlightened; unenthusiastic; unenvious; unfair; unfaithful; unfamiliar; unfazed; unfearing; unfeeling; unfocused; unforgiven; unforgiving; ungallant; ungenerous; unglamorous; ungracious; ungrateful; unguarded; unguilty; unhappy; unheard; unheroic; unholy; unimaginative; unimportant; unimpressed; unified; uninformed; uninhibited; uninspired; unintelligent; uninterested; unique; unkind; unknown; unloved; unmerciful; unmotivated; unmoved; unnerved; unperturbed; unpleasant; unpredictable; unprepared; unproductive; unprotected; unrepentant; unreserved; unresponsive; unrestrained; unromantic; unruffled; unsafe; unsatisfied; unscrupulous; unselfconscious; unselfish; unsettled; unshaken; unsociable; unsteady; unsuccessful; unsupported; unsure; unsurprised; unsympathetic; unthreatened; untrusted; untrusting; unvirtuous; unwanted; unwelcome; unwilling; unwise; uplifted; upset; used; used up; useless.

U – Nouns

ugliness; unaffectedness; unambitiousness; unamiableness; unashamedness; unattractiveness; unbalance; unbelievability; uncertainty; uncheerfulness; uncomfortability; uncouthness; undauntedness; underestimation; understandingness; undeservingness; undignifiedness; uneasiness; unemotionality; unenlightenment; unenthusiasm; unenviousness; unfairness; unfaithfulness; unfamiliarity; unfearingness; unfeelingness; unfocusedness; unforgivingness; ungenerousness; unglamorousness; ungraciousness; ungratefulness; unguardedness; unguiltiness; unhappiness; unheroicness; unholiness; unimaginativeness; unimportance; uninformedness; uninhibitedness; uninspiredness; unintelligence; uninterest; uniqueness; unity; unkindness; unmercifulness; unmotivatedness; unpleasantness; unpredictability; unpreparedness; unproductivity / unproductiveness; unprotectedness; unrepentance; unreservedness; unresponsiveness; unrestrainedness; unsafeness; unsatisfaction; unscrupulousness; unselfconsciousness; unselfishness; unsettledness; unsociability; unsteadiness; unsuccessfulness; unsupportedness; unsureness; unsurprisedness; unsympatheticness; untrustfulness; unvirtuousness; unwantedness; unwelcomeness; unwillingness; unwiseness; upliftedness; uselessness.

V – Adjectives

vacant; vacuous; vain; vainglorious; valiant; valued; vehement; vengeful; venomous; vexed; vibrant; vicious; victimized; victorious; vigilant; villainous; vindicated; vindictive; violated; violent; virtuous; vital; vivacious; volatile; voracious; vulnerable.

V – Nouns

vacancy; vacuity; vainglory; valiance; vanity; vehemence; vengeance; venom; vexation; vibrancy; viciousness; victimization; victory; vigilance; villainy; vindication; violation; violence; virtue; vitality; vivacity; volatility; voracity; vulnerability.

W – Adjectives

wacky; wanted; warm; wary; weak; weary; weepy; weird; well; whimsical; whiny; wicked; wild; willful; wise; wishful; wishy-washy; wistful; withdrawn; witty; woeful; wolfish; wonderful; woozy; worn out; worried; worthless; worthy; wounded; wound up; wrathful; wretched; wronged.

W – Nouns

wackiness; wariness; warmness; weakness; weariness; weirdness; well-being; whimsy; wickedness; wildness; willfulness; wishfulness; wistfulness; withdrawal; woe; wolfishness; wonder; wooziness; worry; worth; worthlessness; wrath; wretchedness.

X – Z – Adjectives

xenophobic; yucky; youthful; zany; zealous; zealless zestless; zesty; zippy; zoned in; zoned out; zonked; zonked out.

X – Z – Nouns / Phrases

yearning (for); yearnings (of); zaniness; zeal; zest.

Emotion: Anger

abrasive; abusive; accusative / accusatory; acrid; acrimonious; aggravated; aggressive; agitated; angry; animalistic; annoyed; antagonistic; antipathetic; apoplectic; argumentative; arrogant; bad-tempered; baleful; ballistic; baneful; barbaric; barbarous; bearish; bellicose; belligerent; berserk; bestial; bilious; bitchy; bitter; bloodthirsty; blustered; boastful; bold; bossy; bratty; brutish; bullish; callous; cantankerous; captious; catty; caustic; chaotic; churlish; coarse; cold; cold-blooded; coldhearted; combative; confrontational; contemptuous; crabby; cranky; critical; cross; cruel; cunning; cynical; dangerous; dark; defiant; demanding; demeaning; demented; depraved; deranged; derisive; despising; destructive; devilish; devious; diabolical; dictatorial; disapproving; disdainful; disgruntled; disharmonious; disobedient; displeased; disrespectful; disruptive; disturbed; dominant; domineering; dour; draconian; edgy; enraged; evil; exacerbated; exploitative; exasperated; explosive; feral; ferocious; fervid; fierce; forceful; fractious; frantic; frenetic; frenzied; fretful; frustrated; furious; galled; glacial; glassy; gloomy; goaded; grouchy; grudging; grumpy; hard-hearted; hacked off; harmful; harried; harsh; hateful; heartless; hostile; hot; hot-headed; hot-tempered; heinous; horrible; hurtful; hypocritical; icy; ill-tempered; indignant; ingenious; infuriated; insane; insensitive; insidious; insolent; insubordinate; intense; intolerant; inconsiderate; irascible; irate; ireful; irked; irritable; insensitive; irritated; livid; loud; mad; malevolent; malicious; maligned; maniacal; masochistic; manipulative; mean; mean-spirited; menacing; merciless; minacious; megalomaniacal; militant; misanthropic; miscreant; monstrous; mordant; murderous; mutinous; mouthy; negative; nasty; obnoxious; ominous; outraged; peevish; patronizing; pessimistic; pettish; petulant; pitiless; pissed; pissed off; powerful; predatory; primitive; pugnacious; pushy; quarrelsome; querulous; rageful; reactionary; reckless; red-hot; refractory; relentless; remorseless; reprochful; resentful; retaliatory; revengeful; riled; rough; rude; ruffled; ruthless; sadistic; sarcastic; sardonic; scornful; sinister; selfish; serious; spiteful; sore; soulless; sour; spirited; spoiled; stern; strict; stubborn; sulky; surly; tantrumy; temperamental; tense; terse; territorial; testy; tetchy; threatening; touchy; tough; tumultuous; tyrannical; unamused; unapologetic; unmerciful; unpleasant; upset; vengeful; venomous; vexed; vicious; victorious; villainous; vindictive; violent; volatile; wicked; wild; wolfish; wrathful.

USAGE EXAMPLES

"Fine," she said, *agitated*. "You can go to hell."

"Close the door on your way out," she said, feeling *bossy*.

"Get away from me," Mary said, *exasperation* in her voice.

"You dare to defy me?" Frank said, *livid* at her refusal.

"I will kill you!" Matthew hissed, *venom* dripping from every word.

Emotion: Fear

afraid; aghast; agitated; alarmed; alert; angsty; antsy; anxious; apprehensive; breathless; bristling; careful; catatonic; cautious; chicken; chilly; circumspect; clammy; claustrophobic; clingy; concerned; constricted; cowardly; creeped out; daunted; defenseless; defensive; despairing; dire; direful; disconcerted; disempowered; distraught; distressed; distrustful; doomed; doubtful; dreadful; emotional; endangered; erratic; exposed; faint; fainthearted; fearful; feeble; fragile; frail; frantic; freaked; freaked out; frenzied; fretful; frightened; grave; guarded; gutless; haggard; harrowed; haunted; helpless; hesitant; hindered; horrified; horror-stricken; hunted; hypervigilant; hysterical; immobile; immobilized; indecisive; intimidated; irrational; jittery; jumpy; menaced; naked; nervous; neurotic; overanxious; overprotective; overwrought; panicked; panicky; paralyzed; paranoid; perturbed; petrified; piteous; pithless; plagued; powerless; precarious; pusillanimous; qualmish; queasy; quivery; rabid; ragged; rattled; reserved; rigid; scared; seized; shaken; shaky; shy; silent; skittish; spineless; spiritless; spooked; squeamish; stalked; stiff; strangled; stressed; stricken; subdued; submissive; suffocated; suspicious; taut; tearful; teary-eyed; tense; tentative; terrorized; threatened; timid; timorous; tingly; tormented; trapped; tremulous; trepid; trepidatious; uncertain; uncontrollable; uneasy; unnerved; unsettled; vigilant; vulnerable; wary; watchful; weak; weepy; worried; xenophobic.

USAGE EXAMPLES

"Please, let me go," he said, looking *alarmed*. "I have a family."

"Is it safe?" Simone said, *concerned.*

Fearful of the distance, she spoke up. "I don't think I can make it."

"We need to find a way out," he said, feeling *overanxious.*

"Did you hear that chair move?" she whispered, *uneasiness* creeping into her voice.

Emotion: Happiness

admiring; adoring; adventurous; affected; amused; animated; avid; beautiful; bemused; blessed; blissful; blithe; bouncy; breezy; bright; bright eyed; brilliant; bubbly; bursting; buzzed; captivated; casual; charged; charismatic; charming; chatty; cheeky; cheerful; cheery; chipper; chirpy; confident; content; contented; convivial; delighted; delightful; dreamy; eager; easy-going; ebullient; ecstatic; effervescent; effusive; elated; emotive; empowered; enamored; enchanted; enchanting; encouraged; encouraging; endearing; energetic; energized; engaged; enhanced; enjoyably; enlivened; enraptured; enriched; entertained; entertaining; enthralled; enthusiastic; entranced; entrancing; esteemed; euphoric; exalted; excellent; excitable; excited; exhilarated; expectant; expressive; extraordinary; extravagant; extroverted; exuberant; exultant; fabulous; fanciful; fancy; fantabulous; fantastic; fervent; festive; flamboyant; flashy; free; frivolous; fulfilled; fun; funky; funloving; funny; gay; genial; genuine; giddy; giggly; glad; glamorous; gleeful; glorious; glowing; glowingly; good; good-natured; goofy; grand; grandiose; grateful; gratified; great; gregarious; groovy; gushy; happy; happy-go-lucky; harmonious; hearty; high; high-spirited; hilarious; humorous; hyped-up; hyper; hyperactive; hysterical; illuminated; incredible; infectious; inspired; invigorated; inviting; jaunty; jazzy; jocular; jolly; jovial; joyful; joyous; jubilant; juiced; keen; kooky; laid back; light-hearted; lively; luminous; magnificent; marvelous; merry; mirthful; momentous; motivated; musical; nice; optimistic; over-enthusiastic; overeager; overjoyed; overzealous; peaceful; peppy; perky; piquant; placid; playful; pleasant; pleased; pleasurable; positive; psyched; pumped (up); quirky; radiant; rapturous; receptive; relaxed; responsive; rhapsodic; sanguine; sensational; serene; silly; sociable; social; special; splendid; sprightly; successful; sunny; super; superb;

superior; swell; talkative; thrilled; tranquil; triumphant; vibrant; victorious; vivacious; voracious; warm; welcoming; well; wonderful; youthful; zany; zealous; zesty; zippy.

USAGE EXAMPLES

"Did you bring it?" Dean asked, *animated.*

"I love it," Lindsey said, *delighted.*

"Of course," she said, feeling *euphoric.*

"I just know he will," Kim said, *optimism* tinging her voice.

Looking and feeling *vibrant,* she introduced herself. "How do you do?"

Emotion: Love

admiring; adoring; affected; affectionate; alluring; altruistic; amative; amorous; appreciated; appreciative; aroused; attached; attracted; bashful; beloved; beneficent; benevolent; besotted; bewitched; blissful; bowled over; breathless; breathtaken; bursting; buzzed; captivated; cared for; carefree; caring; carried away; charismatic; charming; cheeky; cherished; chivalrous; clingy; codependent; comfy; committed; compassionate; compatible; compelled; complete; concerned; connected; considerate; consumed; coy; cozy; cuddly; cute; dashing; debonair; desirable; desired; desirous; desperate; devoted; devout; emotional; empathetic; enamored; enchanted; enchanting; endeared; endearing; enraptured; enticed; enticing; entranced; entrancing; enveloped; envied; ethereal; euphoric; fabulous; faithful; fervent; flirtatious; fond; forlorn; friendly; frisky; gentle; genuine; giddy; giving; glowing; good-looking; good-natured; gorgeous; graceful; gracious; grateful; gratified; gushy; handsome; harmonious; heartfelt; heartful; hearty; helpful; horny; humane; infatuated; intimate; inviting; irresistible; keen; kind; kindhearted; kinky; lascivious; licentious; longing; loved; lovelorn; lovely; lovestruck; loving; loyal; lustful; lusty; maternal; mesmerized; motherly; mushy; needed; needy; nice; nostalgic; nurtured; nurturing; obsessed; obsessive; overprotective; passionate; paternal; peaceful; playful; pleasant; pleased; pleasurable; positive; possessive; pouty; precious; pretty; primal; prized; promiscuous; protected; protective; randy; rapturous; raunchy; ravished;

ravishing; regarded; romantic; sappy; saucy; seduced; seductive; selfless; sensitive; sensual; sensuous; sentimental; sexy; sincere; smitten; smothered; soft-hearted; soothed; soulful; speechless; spellbound; stimulated; suave; supported; supportive; sweet; sympathetic; tantalized; tempestuous; tempted; thankful; thoughtful; thrilled; tingly; tolerant; touched; trusted; trusting; trustworthy; truthful; turned on; understanding; wanted; warm; welcoming; wonderful; worshipful.

USAGE EXAMPLES

"Come here, dear," he said, *affection* in his voice.

"You're as beautiful as ever," Gary said, *bewitched*.

"Your son is handsome," she said, *enraptured*.

Mesmerized, she replied, "Is he single?"

"Thank you," she said, *touched* by the man's kindness.

Emotion: Sadness

abandoned; abysmal; aggrieved; agonized; aimless; alone; anguished; bereaved; bitter; bleak; blue; brittle; broken; broken down; brokenhearted; broken up; broody; browbeaten; bullied; bummed; bummed out; burdened; burdensome; burned out; chagrined; cheerless; choked up; cold; crappy; crestfallen; crummy; crushed; cursed; cut; cut down; cut off; cynical; damaged; damned; dark; dashed; daunted; dead; defeated; defective; deflated; deformed; dejected; demoralized; depressed; desolate; despairing; desperate; despondent; destroyed; detested; devalued; devastated; dire; direful; disappointed; discarded; discomforted; disconcerted; disconnected; discontent; discontented; discordant; discouraged; discriminated; disempowered; disenchanted; disenfranchised; disfavored; disgraced; disharmonious; disheartened; disillusioned; disliked; dismayed; disowned; dispirited; displaced; displeased; disposable; disregarded; dissatisfied; distant; distraught; distressed; disturbed; doleful; dolorous; doomed; dour; down; downcast; downhearted; downtrodden; dragged down; dreadful; dreary; droll; droopy; dull; dulled; emotional; empty; erratic; faithless; fatalistic;

feeble; forsaken; forgotten; forlorn; foul; fragile; frail; friendless; futile; ghastly; gloomy; glum; grave; gray / grey; grief-stricken; grim; gutted; hapless; harried; hated; haunted; heartbroken; heartrending; heartsick; heavy-hearted; helpless; hollow; homesick; hopeless; horrible; humiliated; hunted; hurt; ignored; imploringly; inferior; invisible; irrational; isolated; joyless; knocked (down); lonesome; longingly; loveless; low; low-spirited; lugubrious; maudlin; melancholic; melodramatic; mirthless; miserable; misunderstood; mocked; moody; mopey; morbid; mournful; moved; nameless; negative; neglected; numb; ostracized; overlooked; oversensitive; overwrought; pained; painful; pathetic; pensive; pessimistic; piteous; pitiful; powerless; purposeless; put down; regretful; rejected; remorseful; remote; resented; resigned; ridiculed; rotten; rueful; ruined; ruthful; sad; self-critical; self-deprecating; self-effacing; self-pitying; sentimental; shaky; shamefaced; shunned; sick at heart; solemn; somber; sore; sorrowful; soulful; sour; spiritless; strained; strangled; stressed; suffering; suicidal; sulky; sullen; tantrumy; tearful; teary-eyed; teased; temperamental; tormented; torn; torturous; touchy; tremulous; troubled; tumultuous; ugly; unattractive; uncared for; uncheerful; unconsolable; uncontrollable; unhappy; unharmonious; unimportant; uninspired; unloved; unmotivated; unreserved; unrestrained; unsettled; unsteady; unsuccessful; unwanted; unwelcome; upset; useless; vacant; vulnerable; weak; wearisome; weary; weepy; whiny; woeful; worthless; wounded; wretched.

USAGE EXAMPLES

"You really don't care, do you?" she cried, *aggrieved* by his lack of empathy.

"Your father didn't return any of my calls," his mother said, looking *dejected*.

"No," I said, *disheartened*. "I can't."

Heartbroken, she sulked, "Why doesn't he love me?"

With *solemnness* her only friend, Kathy replied, "Life is black like my heart."

Emotion: Surprise

aghast; agog; alarmed; alert; amazed; astonished; astounded; awed; awesome; awestruck; baffled; bamboozled; bedazzled; befuddled; bewildered; blown away; bowled over; breathtaken; caught out; dazzled; fainthearted; flabbergasted; flummoxed; gobsmacked; hoodwinked; horrified; hysterical; incredulous; jarred; jolted; jumpy; mesmerized; mystified; outraged; overwhelmed; perplexed; puzzled; quizzical; shaken; shaky; shocked; speechless; spellbound; startled; stunned; stupefied; suckered; surprised; tremulous.

USAGE EXAMPLES

"I don't know why," he said, *aghast.*

"Is it true?" he whispered with *astonishment.*

Bewildered, Susan asked, "What the hell is that thing?"

"I don't know what to make of it," Dave said, *perplexed.*

She was *speechless.* "I never thought I'd live to see the day."

Emotion: Unfeeling

aloof; amoral; apathetic; barefaced; bland; blank; blunt; bold; bored; brazen; brisk; calculating; candid; carefree; careless; casual; cavalier; cheerless; clear-headed; closed; closed off; cold; cold-blooded; cold-hearted; composed; conservative; constrained; cool; critical; cynical; dauntless; detached; devil-may-care; dimensionless; direct; disconnected; disinterested; dismissive; dispassionate; disrespectful; distant; elusive; emotionless; empty; flat; forward; frank; grounded; guiltless; hard-hearted; hardened; heartless; hollow; humorless; icy; impassive; impermeable; imperturbable; impervious; indifferent; ingenuous; inhumane; inscrutable; insensitive; insincere; insouciant; intolerant; irreproachable; joyless; laconic; languid; lifeless; mirthless; mundane; needless; neglectful; negligent; neutral; nonchalant; noncommittal; numb; passionless; passive; pessimistic; resigned; shameless; sober;

stable; stoic; stolid; unaffected; unapologetic; uncaring; unemotional; unfeeling; vacant; wolfish.

USAGE EXAMPLES

"Whatever you say, sunshine," he said, *barefaced.*

"The day is almost done," Grace said, feeling *cheerless.*

"Um, sure," she replied, *distant.*

Nonchalant, Penny said, "I don't see the problem."

"Get over yourself," he said, *unfeeling.*

Physical State: Hungry / Thirsty

arid; avaricious; avid; breathless; carnivorous; covetous; deprived; desirous; eager; empty; esurient; faint; famished; gluttonous; greedy; hoggish; hollow; hungry; insatiable; insatiate; keen; lightheaded; peaky; peckish; piggish; rapacious; ravenous; slothful; starved; starving; thirsty; unfilled; unquenchable; unsatisfied; voracious; yearning.

USAGE EXAMPLES

Avaricious, he asked the waiter, "Can I get a large steak?"

"I can't go on," he croaked, *famished* and out of breath.

Lightheaded, Vince beckoned her over. "I require sustenance."

Looking *ravenous*, one of the men yelled, "Don't keep us waiting."

"Help me," he said, with a look of *starvation* in his eyes.

Physical State: Sick

abysmal; afflicted; agonized; awful; bleak; blighted; broken down; chilly; clammy; cold; crappy; crippled; crummy; dazed; debilitated; delirious; dismal; dizzy; drunk; enfeebled; faint; feeble; feverish; flush; foul; fragile; frail; frigid; hazy; hot; hung over; ill; impaired; inebriated; intoxicated; lame; lifeless; lightheaded; limp; lousy; low; nauseous; pained; painful; paralyzed; plagued; poisoned; poorly; queasy; rotten; rough; shaky; sick; sluggish; sore; squeamish; strained; strangled; stressed; stricken; struck down; suffering; tearful; teary-eyed; tingly; tipsy; tormented; tremulous; weak; weepy; woeful; woozy; wretched.

USAGE EXAMPLES

Debilitated as he was, Lance still managed to issue a warning. "They are almost upon us."

"I can see angels in the sky," the man said, *delirious*.

Feeling *feverish*, she whimpered, "I need more medicine."

A wave of *nausea* suddenly overcame her. "Please, we must hurry."

"I'm sorry," he said, feeling slightly *queasy*. "I can't eat that."

Physical State: Tired

absent-minded; asleep; beat; bleary-eyed; buggered; burned out; catatonic; comatose; crabby; cranky; depleted; dizzy; drained; drowsy; dull; effete; empty; exhausted; faint; fallow; fatigued; flat; foggy; frazzled; fried; groggy; grouchy; grumpy; haggard; irritated; knackered; knocked out; lackadaisical; lackluster; lazy; lethargic; listless; moody; numb; overworked; petered out; punch drunk; ragged; run down; sedate; serene; sleepy; slow; sluggish; soporific; spent; tired; tranquil; used up; vacant; weary; winded; withdrawn; zealless; zestless; zoned out; zonked; zonked out.

"Are we almost done?" she asked, feeling *burned out*.

Drained, Michelle motioned toward the bed. "I'm going to get some sleep."

"I can't do this anymore," he said, *fatigued*.

"I want to go home," she said with a hint of *moodiness*.

Feeling *spent*, Ryan headed for the door. "I'm going to get a few hours shuteye."

Manner: Bored

absent; adrift; aimless; alone; aloof; apathetic; asleep; banal; bland; blank; blasé; bleak; blue; bored; caged in; catatonic; cheerless; cloistered; closed off; comatose; confined; cooped up; cut off; dark; dead; debilitated; deflated; demotivated; depressed; despondent; detached; disconnected; disinterested; distant; distracted; diverted; dull; excluded; fidgety; gloomy; glum; gray / grey; halfhearted; idle; immobile; immobilized; inactive; incapacitated; indifferent; irritable; isolated; joyless; lackadaisical; lackluster; lame; languid; lazy; lethargic; lifeless; limp; listless; low; low-spirited; moody; mopey; mundane; numb; paralyzed; passionless; passive; perfunctory; remote; removed; resigned; restless; sedate; sedated; slack; slow; sluggish; spiritless; stuporous; subdued; unambitious; unconcerned; unenthusiastic; unexcited; unfocused; uninquisitive; uninspired; uninterested; unmotivated; unmoved; unproductive; unresponsive; vacant; weary; withdrawn; zoned out.

USAGE EXAMPLES

"I don't remember," he said, *apathetic*.

"I wish he would," she said, *despondent*. "Things around here are so dull."

"Do whatever you want," he replied, *disinterested* in her plight.

Idle and *uninspired*, Simone said, "I couldn't be bothered."

With a look of *resignation* on her face, Catherine said, "Sometimes, I wish I'd never wake up again."

Manner: Confused

absent; absent-minded; absurdly; addled; aimless; ambivalent; asinine; baffled; bamboozled; bedazzled; bedeviled; befuddled; bewildered; blank; blind; boggled; brainless; capricious; clouded; clueless; confounded; confused; daft; dazed; delirious; deluded; demented; dense; deranged; dim; dimwitted; discombobulated; disconcerted; disorganized; disoriented; ditzy; doubtful; dubious; dull; dumb; dumbfounded; dumbstruck; erratic; fatuous; flummoxed; foggy; foolish; forgetful; fragmented; garbled; glib; hazy; idiotic; ignorant; impaired; inane; incoherent; incompetent; indecisive; inept; inexactly; irrational; jumbled; lost; mindless; misguided; misinformed; moronic; morose; muddied; muddled; murky; mystified; naive; oblivious; perplexed; puzzled; quizzical; scatterbrained; scattered; senile; simple; slow; struck dumb; stupid; thickheaded; unclever; uncritical; unenlightened; uninformed; unintelligent; unknowingly; unsure; unwise; vacuous; witless.

USAGE EXAMPLES

"Is that really what he said?" he asked, *baffled*.

Confounded, Michael spoke for the first time. "I still don't understand what it means."

Discombobulated by their sudden exit, Marcy asked, "Was it something I said?"

"Your brother is really strange," she said, *dumbfounded* by Carl's erratic behavior.

Sorry," she said *scatterbrained*, "but where is the bathroom again?"

Manner: Critical

admonishing; adversarial; analytical; appraising; approving; argumentative; assessing; belittled; berated; biased; blamed; captious; censored; challenged; condemning; condescending; constructive; correct; critical; cynical; demanding; demeaning; denounced; derided; derisive; disapproved of; disapproving; disbelieving; discerning; discouraging; discriminating; disfavorable; dismissive; disparaging; doubtful; examined; fastidious; fickle; finicky; frank; fussy; hypocritical; impartial; intolerant; judgmental; judicious; logical; nagging; narrow-minded; nit-picky; objective; opinionated; opposing; overcritical; patronizing; pessimistic; picky; prejudiced; priggish; pushy; reproachful; sardonic; scornful; self-critical; self-deprecating; self-effacing; skeptical; slanderous; terse; unbelieving; unbiased; unconvinced; unemotional.

USAGE EXAMPLES

"You don't strike me as the type," she said, her eyes *appraising*.

"Well," he said with an air of *condescension*, "nobody's perfect."

"Jonathan," Helen said, *disapproving*. "You mustn't talk that way about your grandmother."

Overcritical of the service, Mr. Jones lashed out. "I demand to see the person in charge at once."

"Oh, I'm sure you tried your best," she said, *skeptical*.

Manner: Deceptive

bamboozled; beguiled; betrayed; bewitched; brainwashed; cagey; cajoled; calculating; caught out; cheated; cheated on; clandestine; coaxed; coerced; compromised; confidential; conflicted; conned; conniving; conspiratorial; conspired against; contrived; controlled; controlling; convinced; covert; cunning; deceitful; deceived; deceptive; devious; disbelieved; disbelieving; dishonest; disingenuous; disloyal; distrusted; distrustful; double-crossed; doubted; doubtful; dubious; duped; evasive; facetious; fake; fallacious; false; farcical; fraudulent;

furtive; guileful; guilty; gypped; hoodwinked; hustled; immoral; incongruent; leery; lied about; lied to; manipulated; manipulative; mischievous; misinformed; misled; mistrusted; mistrustful; morally bankrupt; opportunistic; ostensible; paranoid; perfidious; persuaded; persuasive; phony; pliable; pliant; predatory; preyed upon; propagandistic; propagandized; remorseless; ruthless; sabotaged; sarcastic; scheming; screwed over; secretive; shifty; shortchanged; shrewd; sinful; sinister; sketchy; slighted; sly; sneaky; stealthy; subversive; suckered; surreptitious; suspicious; swindled; tactical; traitorous; treacherous; treasonous; tricky; twisted; underhanded; unfaithful; unreliable; unrepentant; unscrupulous; untruthful; unvirtuous; wily; wolfish.

USAGE EXAMPLES

Feeling *conned*, he bellowed, "Why, that crooked bastard!"

"I hope for your sake it's true," he said with an expression of *doubt*.

Feeling *hustled*, she spoke up. "I want my money back, thief!"

"A gin and tonic," Gavin ordered, *leery* of the woman's watchful eyes.

Being *underhanded*, he whispered, "Give me the key to his apartment."

Manner: Disgusted

abhorred; abhorrent; crude; defiled; despicable; detestable; dirty; disgusted; disgusting; execrated; fetid; filthy; foul; freakish; fulsome; ghastly; gross; grotesque; gruesome; icky; indecent; indecorous; lewd; licentious; loath; loathed; loathing; loathsome; macabre; monstrous; nauseated; obscene; offensive; perverse; perverted; poisonous; putrid; queasy; rancid; repelled; repugnant; repulsed; repulsive; revolted; revolting; rotten; salacious; shocking; sick; sickened; sleazy; slimy; sordid; squeamish; vile; vulgar; wicked.

USAGE EXAMPLES

"You're not sorry," John said, *disgusted* with him.

Feeling *loathsome*, she replied, "I won't be here much longer."

Nauseated, the child said, "I can't bare to look at you."

"Keep it away from me," she said with a look of *repugnance*.

Sensing his *vile* stare, she whimpered, "Please, let me go."

Manner: Embarrassed

abashed; awkward; bashful; clammy; demure; disconcerted; embarrassed; flush; flustered; frigid; humiliated; jittery; judged; mortified; nervous; overanxious; self-conscious; shaken; shaky; shamed; shameful; sheepish; shy; skittish; squeamish; stunned; surprised; timid; traumatized; tremulous; uncomfortable; uneasy; unnerved; vulnerable.

USAGE EXAMPLES

"Do you like it here?" he asked, slightly *bashful*.

"I didn't realize someone was in here," Dave said, *embarrassed*.

"Please forgive me," Mary said, with a look of *humiliation* on her face.

Feeling *shamed*, she protested. "I didn't do anything wrong!"

Uncomfortable at the mere suggestion, he replied, "Of course not."

Manner: Jealous

accusative; accusatory; accusing; adversarial; anxious; argumentative; avaricious; begrudged; besmirched; bitchy; bitter; bratty; brooding; callous; callow; catty; childish; competitive; confrontational; conniving; contemptible; contemptuous; coveted; covetous; cunning; demanding; desperate; devious; dictatorial; disapproving; doubtful; embittered; emotional; envious; fixated; forlorn; greedy; grudging; guarded; hateful; hostile; immature; infatuated; insecure; intimidated; intrusive; irrational;

jaded; jealous; jilted; leery; longing; lovelorn; manipulative; melodramatic; mistrustful; neurotic; nosy; nutty; overprotective; paranoid; paternal; petty; possessed; possessive; protective; psychopathic; psychotic; pushy; resentful; scandalous; scorned; scornful; selfish; solicitous; sour; spiteful; stalked; suspicious; threatening; unfaithful; unromantic; untrusting; vigilant; wary; watchful; worried; wounded; wrathful; zealous.

USAGE EXAMPLES

"I want to see your phone," Marcy said, *argumentative* now.

"Give it to me right now!" she said in a fit of *childishness*.

"Don't worry yourself, dear," he replied, a hint of *deviousness* in his voice.

"Is he rich?" he asked her, clearly showing his *insecurity*.

Jealous of his new girlfriend, Amanda whispered: "Does she really think those shoes look good on her?"

Manner: Pandering

abiding; accessible; accommodating; acknowledging; affirmative; affirming; agreeable; amenable; amicable; apologetic; appeasing; assenting; complaisant; compliant; complicit; complimentary; compromised; congenial; conservative; considerate; contained; convivial; cooperative; credulous; devoted; docile; doted on; doting; dutiful; flattered; friendly; generous; genial; good-natured; hospitably; idolized; ingratiated; inviting; loyal; obedient; obliged; obliging; obsequious; pandering; parasitic; passive; peaceable; permissive; pious; placated; pliable; propitious; receptive; reciprocative; selfless; servile; sincere; slavish; smarmy; submissive; subservient; supplicating; supportive; sycophantic; unimposing; uxorious; venerative; worshipful.

USAGE EXAMPLES

Feeling *amicable*, Arthur replied, "I didn't mean anything by it."

"I only want what's best for you, sir," she said, trying her best to *appease* him.

Compliant to his wishes, she responded, "Very well, I'll have it sorted out immediately."

"I will fetch your coat," he said with *docility*.

Slavish and *sycophantic*, Ronald said, "You will always be my top priority."

Manner: Polite

abiding; accepting; accessible; accommodating; acknowledging; affable; amiable; appreciative; charming; chatty; chivalrous; civil; classy; communicative; complimentary; considerate; conversational; cordial; courteous; courtly; cultivated; cultured; deferential; formal; friendly; genial; genteel; good-natured; gracious; hospitable; inviting; kind; kindhearted; mannerly; mild-mannered; modest; nice; obeisant; obliging; polite; respected; respectful; sociable; thankful; thoughtful; unimposing; warm; welcoming; well-mannered; well-meaning.

USAGE EXAMPLES

"So, Jerry," he said, trying his best to remain *civil*, "what is it you do?"

Feeling *complimentary*, she motioned to her dress. "What a lovely garment, Lucy."

"Thank you, sir," Harry said, *gracious* as usual.

Showing great *hospitality*, he said, "Would you care to join us?"

With *kindness*, she consoled the old man. "I'm so sorry for your loss."

Manner: Proud / Austere

accomplished; almighty; ambitious; aristocratic; arrogant; assertive; audacious; auspicious; austere; authoritative; autocratic; autonomous; boastful; bold; bossy; cavalier; charismatic; charming; chauvinistic; cocky; commanding; complacent; conceitedly; condescending; confident; courtly; cultivated; cultured; dapper; debonair; decorous; despotic; devious; dictatorial; dignified; direct; distinguished; dominant; domineering; draconian; dutiful; egocentric; egotistical; elegant; elite; eminent; exalted; extroverted; flamboyant; flashy; flawless; foppish; forceful; gaudy; glamorous; grand; grandiose; haughty; immodest; imperious; important; indulgent; infallible; influential; intelligent; invincible; invulnerable; knightly; knowledgeable; lofty; magisterial; magnanimous; masterful; narcissistic; noble; obnoxious; opinionated; oppressive; opulent; ostentatious; outspoken; overconfident; patriotic; patronizing; peremptory; perfect; perfectionistic; pompous; powerful; prestigious; pretentious; prideful; prissy; privileged; prodigious; prosperous; proud; puissant; refined; regal; righteous; royal; sanctimonious; satisfied; self-absorbed; self-approving; self-assured; self-centered; self-confident; self-important; self-interested; self-possessed; self-righteous; self-satisfied; showy; smug; snobbish; snobby; snooty; sophisticated; stuck up; stylish; suave; supercilious; superior; triumphant; tyrannical; unctuous; urbane; vain; vainglorious; victorious.

USAGE EXAMPLES

"Ignore it," he said, *authoritative*. "Now, follow me."

Confident now, Lauren said, "Hand me my phone."

Haughty and full of liquor, she laughed. "You silly little urchin."

With *pretentious* vigor, he replied, "Well, we demand only the best for our children."

"It's a good thing I'm here then, isn't it?" Henry said, a *vainglorious* smirk crossing his lips.

Manner: Rude

abrasive; abusive; affronted; antisocial; argumentative; bad-mannered; barbaric; barbarous; bitchy; boorish; bossy; brash; bratty; brutish; caddish; cantankerous; careless; chauvinistic; coarse; combative; condescending; defamatory; defiant; demanding; deplorable; discourteous; dismissive; disobedient; disobliging; disrespectful; disruptive; flippant; impatient; impertinent; impolite; imprudent; impudent; impulsive; inconsiderate; indecorous; indignant; insensitive; insincere; insolent; insubordinate; insulted; intruded upon; lewd; libelous; loutish; mouthy; nosy; obscene; patronizing; pushy; querulous; rash; rude; snide; snubbed; surly; tactless; tasteless; terse; thankless; thoughtless; unamiable; unapologetic; unceremonious; uncharitable; uncivil; uncommunicative; uncordial; uncouth; ungenerous; ungenial; ungracious; ungrateful; unharmonious; uninhibited; unkind; unpleasant; unprofessional; unrefined; unwelcoming.

USAGE EXAMPLES

Revealing her *abusive* nature, Katie hissed: "You look ugly in that shirt."

"Keep your questions to yourself!" David replied in a *brutish* manner.

"Get your facts straight," he said in a *coarse* tone.

"I refuse to answer any more questions," she said, feeling *insulted*.

"I thought your wife had blonde hair," said *tactless* Kimberly.

Manner: Serious / Rational

academic; amoral; analytical; assertive; astute; authoritative; brainy; candid; civil; competent; composed; conscientious; critical; decisive; deductive; diligent; diplomatic; direct; eloquent; enlightened; erudite; experienced; formal; forthright; forward; frank; frugal; geeky; grounded; helpful; illuminated; important; informative; ingenious; instructive; intelligent; intense; intent; interrogative; judicious; knowledgeable; laconic; learned; lenient; logical; mature; meditative; methodical; meticulous; militaristic; mindful; moral; observant; passionless; patient;

pedantic; perspicacious; philosophical; political; practical; pragmatic; professional; proficient; prosaic; purposeful; qualified; rational; realistic; reasonable; responsible; restrained; sagacious; sagely; scholastic; scientific; sensible; serious; shrewd; skillful; smart; sober; staunch; steadfast; stern; stoic; stolid; strategic; strict; studious; tense; terse; unamused; unfazed; wise.

USAGE EXAMPLES

With the *astuteness* of a scholar, Jonathan reasoned, "Is this not a matter of perception?"

"You can't be that blind," he said, *direct* and to the point.

"The best way to infiltrate is to use a known benefactor," she said, *knowledgeable* about the group's inner workings.

Observant, David asked, "Isn't there a possibility of overload?"

Shrewd and *unfazed*, Helen said, "I gladly accept your proposal."

Manner: Stubborn

adamant; anarchic; antagonistic; antisocial; argumentative; bossy; bratty; bullheaded; cantankerous; close-minded; combative; contumacious; defiant; determined; disagreeable; disobedient; dogged; dogmatic; formidable; hard-headed; imperious; impertinent; implacable; inflexible; intransigent; mulish; mutinous; noncompliant; nonconforming; obstinate; obstreperous; obtrusive; offensive; opinionated; opposed; persevering; persistent; petulant; pigheaded; rebellious; recalcitrant; refractory; resolute; resolved; rigid; singleminded; stubborn; territorial; unbending; uncompliant; uncompromising; uncooperative; unreceptive; unrelenting; unshakable; unwavering; unwilling; unyielding; willful.

USAGE EXAMPLES

"You need to stay out of my business," she said in a *bossy* tone of voice.

"Leave my stuff alone," he said, *cantankerous*.

"Give it your best shot, buddy," the old man said, *determined* to stand his ground.

Feeling *rebellious*, Alison let loose. "You're not going to tell me what to do!"

"I'm not leaving without it," Martin said, *uncooperative*.

Manner: Truthful

believable; candid; conspicuous; correct; faithful; forthright; frank; genuine; guileless; honest; ingenuous; innocent; just; justified; kosher; open; outspoken; realistic; reliable; righteous; scrupulous; sincere; trusting; trustworthy; truthful; unaffected; unreserved; virtuous.

USAGE EXAMPLES

"I'm telling you the truth," he said, trying to sound *genuine*.

With an *innocent* look on her face, she said, "I think you're confusing me with someone else."

Feeling *righteous*, Eric replied, "There are people here tonight who are trying to deceive you."

"No harm will come to you while I'm around," he said with *sincerity*.

"I would never do such a thing," she said, *virtuous*.

Modifying Words

broadcasting; burying; cloaking; concealing; covering up; disguising; displaying; disregarding; exhibiting; exposing; exuding; feeling; giving off; gripped by; harboring; hiding; hinting (about/at/that); holding back; ignoring; in; masking; oozing; quashing; radiating; revealing; showing; smothering; sounding; squashing; stifling; suppressing; with.

USAGE EXAMPLES

"I'm so happy for you both," she said, *concealing* her bitterness.

"Their flight is late," he said, *feeling* nervous.

"You're amazing, Judy," she said *in* awe.

"We still have a few more minutes," Jay said, *sounding* anxious.

"I can't wait to see them," she said *with* enthusiasm.

Internal Dialogue and Thought Tags

acknowledged; agonized over; believed; boiled; bristled; brooded; cerebrated; cogitated; conceptualized; concluded; considered; contemplated; daydreamed; decided; deduced; deliberated; doubted; dwelled upon; envisioned; evaluated; examined; fancied; fantasized; figured; fretted; fumed; fussed; hoped; imagined; introspected; knew; lamented; meditated on; moped; mulled over; mused; perceived; pictured; planned; pondered; puzzled over; questioned; rationalized; realized; reasoned; reflected; regarded; repined; ruminated; schemed; seethed; speculated; stewed over; studied; sulked; theorized; thought; vexed; visualized; wondered.

USAGE EXAMPLES

Perhaps it's for the best, she *concluded*.

He *considered* what this all meant.

Jane *doubted* he'd really go through with it.

For a moment, she *pondered* whether she should avoid him at the dance.

Was this injury going to lead to his retirement? Michael *wondered*.

4
Body Language and Movement

Body Language and *movement* phrases help a reader to feel more of what a character is going through. There is an engaging quality to this form a writing that straight dialogue can't match.

Arms

he caught her up in his arms

he put his arms around her

he said, cradling her in his arms

he said, drawing her into his arms

he said, folding his arms across his chest

he said, folding his arms defiantly

he said, his arms (dropping/falling) to his sides

he said, his arm slackening from around her

he said, his arms tightly around her

he said, swinging her up in his arms

he said as he lifted her into his arms

he swept her up in his arms

he touched her arm

he withdrew his arm from around her waist

his arms tightened around her

she attempted to pull away from him, but his arm tightened around her

she felt him slide his arm around her waist

she rubbed the goosebumps from her arms

she said, brushing his arm away

she said, clutching his arm

she said, cuddling her arms around her body

she said, folding her arms behind her head

she said, her arms crossed over her chest

she said, her arms encircling his neck

she said, her arms folded defiantly across her chest

she said, her arms spreading wide

she said, raising her arms in surrender

she said, raising her arms over her head

USAGE EXAMPLES

"Everything is going to be fine," *he said, drawing her into his arms.*

His arms tightened around her. "You're not going anywhere."

"Don't leave me alone with her," *she said, clutching his arm.*

Arms: Fingers

he asked, his fingers seeking the (...)

he closed her fingers over the (...)

he ordered with a snap of his fingers

her fingers clenched

her fingers curled around his

her fingers wrenched free of his

he said, his fingers pressing into her tender flesh

he said, his fingers tightening on hers

he said, his fingertips traveling down her arm to her hand

he said, pointing a finger at (...)

he snapped his fingers

his fingers brushed her arm

his fingers closed around hers

his fingers dug into her

his fingers gripped her chin

his fingers gripped hers

his fingers gripped hers as she tried to pull away

his fingers gripped her wrist tightly

his fingers slid down her arm, leaving their warmth on her skin

his fingers slid down to her wrist

his fingers tightened on her arm

his lean fingers enclosed hers

she said, her fingernails digging into his (arm/back/shoulder)

she stroked a finger against his cheek

she touched a finger to (...)

she touched her fingertips to (her/his) lips

she traced a fingertip over (...)

USAGE EXAMPLES

"Would you like a drink?" *he asked, his fingers seeking the* light switch.

He snapped his fingers. "Charles, get me a drink."

His fingers gripped her wrist tightly. "I need you here with me."

Arms: Hands / Palms

as she spoke, he placed his strong hands on her waist

he extended a hand

he handed her a (...)

he held out his right hand

he held up a hand

he lifted a hand and removed his sunglasses

he raised a hand and stroked his jaw

he reached out a hand

he reached out and took her firmly by the hand

he rested a hand on her arm

her fingernails dug into the palms of her hands

her hands clenched into fists

her hands crept together in her lap

her hands gripped each other (in her lap)

her hand shook as she reached for it

he said, handing her (...)

he said, his hands gripping (...)

he said, holding out a hand

he said, holding out his palm

he said, throwing out a hand toward (...)

he stretched out a beckoning hand

he swept a hand around the room

he took her by the hand

he took hold of her (left/right) hand

his hands thrust into the pockets of his (...)

his hands tightened on her arms

his hands took hold of hers

she broke into tears and buried her face in her hands

she buried her face in her hands

she could feel her hand shaking

she extended a hand across the table

she felt her palms growing clammy

she felt his hand cup her elbow

she held out a hand to him and he took it

she placed the (object) in his palm

she raised her hand in protest

she rested a hand on her hip

she said, clenching her hands at her sides

she said, handing him a (...)

she said, her palms growing clammy

she said, letting go of his hand

she said, shaking his hand

she spread her hands

she stood there with her hands in the pockets of her (...)

she waved a hand

she waved a hand towards the (...)

withdrawing her hand from his, she said

USAGE EXAMPLES

He extended a hand. "Come with me."

"Take your excuses elsewhere." *Her hands clenched into fists.*

"Are you sure no one else is here?" *She felt her palms growing clammy.*

Body

a (burst/rush) of heat ran over her body

a cold sweat filmed her body

a cold tremor ran through her body

a rush of (emotion) stormed through her body

a shiver of emotion ran through her body

a shiver ran through her body

as she stood there a tremor shook her body

a tremor shook her body

(emotion) stirred through her body

every fiber of her body was taut with (emotion)

every nerve in her body seemed to (cry out/shrink)

he felt (emotion) in every fiber of his body

he felt as if every single muscle in his body was on fire

he felt a sudden chill sweep through his body

he let his gaze wander slowly down her body

her body felt as if it was floating

her body felt as if it were on fire

her body felt cold

her body reacted to his words

her body tensed

her body tensed and her mind cried a warning

her body was rigid with tension

her body went rigid hearing the words

her body went tense with shock

her entire body was vibrating to the thump of her heart

her heart thumped and a quiver ran through her body

her nerves tingled throughout her body

her tired body slumped against (...)

he said, his body pressing against hers

he said, pressing her close to the warmth of his body

he said, pressing her to his body

his entire body seemed to tauten

his touch moved down her body to her hand

pain shot upwards through her body

panic spread through her body

perspiration pricked his body

she felt (emotion) with every atom of her body

she felt a draining weakness in her body

she felt as if an electric current had shot through her body

she felt as if something twisted in her body

she felt a sudden angry trembling through her body

she felt herself trembling all through her body

she felt the blood rise in a wave of heat through her body

she let her body sag against his

she said, her body brushing against his for a moment

she said, her body drenched in sweat

she said, her body growing (clammy/cold)

she said, her body inclining towards him

she said, her body pulsing with nervous energy

she tensed all through her body as he (...)

she twisted her body to look at him

she whispered, her body trembling uncontrollably in his arms

the (sentence/words) sent panic signals racing through her body

USAGE EXAMPLES

A cold tremor ran through her body. "What do you want from me?"

"You repulse me!" *He felt hatred in every fiber of his body.*

"Pretty please," *she said, her body inclining towards him.*

Body: Heart

a hand of fear clutched at her heart

as she spoke she felt a strange lurch of her heart

her heart beat fast from a combination of fear and excitement

her heart beat fast with apprehension

her heartbeats quickened

her heart filled with emotion

her heart fluttered wildly

her heart gave a lurch

her heart gave a nervous jolt

her heart gave a twist in her chest

her heart leapt with joy

her heart pounded beneath her rib cage

her heart sank

her heart seemed as if it had come into her throat

her heart seemed to plummet into the pit of her stomach

her heart seemed to turn over

her heart shook at the word

her heart skipped a beat (as he spoke)

her heart was a hammer beating in her chest

her heart was beating so fast that she was breathless

her heart was pounding as she (...)

her heart was racing

he said, his heart beating fast

he said, his heart bounding with pleasure

he said, his heart bursting with joy

he said, his heart drumming against his ribs

his heart began to beat more rapidly

she asked, though in her heart she already knew the answer

she clutched a hand to her heart

she could feel her heart beating so fast it made her feel faint and breathless

she could feel her heart beating strangely fast as (...)

she could feel the thudding of her heart

she felt her heart beating with apprehension

she felt her heart give a leap

she said, and she was wishing with all her heart that (...)

she said, feeling her heart fill with (emotion)

she said, feeling her heart skip a beat

she said, her heart breaking

she said, her heart sinking as she realized (...)

she said, her heart so full of love she thought it would explode

she said, her heart swelling with emotion

she said with her heart in her throat

USAGE EXAMPLES

"Thank you." *Her heart fluttered wildly.*

"I want to marry you!" *he said, his heart bursting with joy.*

"May I sit down," *she said with her heart in her throat.*

Body: Shoulders

he caught hold of her shoulders and held her back

he frowned, then shrugged his shoulders

he gave a dismissive shrug of his shoulders

he gave her shoulder an encouraging squeeze

he gripped her by the shoulder

he laid a hand on her trembling shoulder

he patted her shoulder rather awkwardly

her fingers clenched his shoulder

her fingers gripped his shoulder

her head moved drowsily against his shoulder

he said, his shoulders slumping

he said over his shoulder

he shrugged his shoulders

he took her by the shoulders

his fingers deliberately caressed her shoulders

his hands caught at her shoulders

his hands closed on her shoulders

his hands slipped from her shoulders

his hands were warm upon her shoulders

his shoulders lifted in a shrug

she called back over her shoulder to him

she cast a frightened glance over her shoulder

she grinned and shrugged a shoulder at him

she punched his shoulder in anger

she said, clenching his shoulder

she said, resting her head against his shoulder

she said, with a shrug of her shoulders

she shrugged her shoulder away from his hand

she smiled against his warm shoulder

she took a hasty glance over her shoulder

USAGE EXAMPLES

He laid a hand on her trembling shoulder. "Try to calm down."

"I'm sick of her lies," *he said, his shoulders slumping.*

"I hate you!" *She punched his shoulder in anger.*

Body: Skin / Flesh

a shiver ran like a ghostly touch over her skin

a shiver ran over her skin

a tiny tremor ran all over her skin

her flesh crawled with sparks of electricity

her skin glowed with a pink hue

her skin grew hot

her skin prickled with alarm

her skin quivered from his touch

her skin tautened as his words fell upon her ears

her skin tightened with goosebumps

her skin tingled at his touch

he said, his breath fanning her skin

he said, his warm breath fanning her skin

he said, nearly jumping out of his skin

he said, touching her warm skin

he spoke the words against her skin

his flesh crawled

she almost jumped out of her skin

she could feel her skin growing paler as he (...)

she could feel her skin warming as he (...)

she felt a flush prickle her skin

she felt a tightening of her skin as he spoke the words

she felt goosebumps rising on her skin

she felt her skin blush with embarrassment

she replied, feeling his warm skin against hers

she said, her flesh crawling with dread

she said, her flesh rippling

she whispered, her skin prickling with fear

the look in his eyes made her skin quiver

the warmth of his mouth moved against her skin

USAGE EXAMPLES

"Is anyone there?" *Her skin prickled with alarm.*

"You smell wonderful," *he said, his breath fanning her skin.*

She felt a flush prickle her skin. "I–I need to be going, sorry."

Body: Spine

a cold shiver ran all the way down her spine

a cold thrill went up and down her spine

a shiver ran the length of her spine

her spine stiffened at the words

her spine tensing when he spoke the words

his voice made her spine stiffen with (emotion)

ice trickled down her spine

nervous prickles ran up her spine

she could feel a stiffening of her spine as he spoke the words

she felt a chill crawl down her spine

she felt a chill that seemed to reach to the very bottom of her spine

she felt a shiver run down her spine

she felt as if drops of ice were running down her spine

she replied, her spine involuntarily stiffening at the prospect

she said, feeling a shiver run up and down her spine

she said, her spine stiffening with indignation

she shivered as cold drops of dread ran down her spine

she snapped, her spine stiffening in outrage

she whispered, her spine stiffening

suddenly her spine stiffened as he spoke behind her

the tone of his voice made her spine stiffen

the words sent nervous chills up and down her spine

USAGE EXAMPLES

"You get no say in the matter." *His voice made her spine stiffen with fear.*

She felt a shiver run down her spine. "I can't believe you would do such a thing!"

"Is anyone there?" *she whispered, her spine stiffening.*

Body: Stomach

a feeling of excitement stirred in the pit of her stomach

a sense of dread rolled through the pit of her stomach

excitement fluttered deep in the pit of her stomach

he felt a clutch of panic in the pit of his stomach

her stomach muscles contracted at his look

her stomach muscles fluttered

he said, guilt blooming in his stomach

he said, uneasiness beginning to stir his stomach

nausea gripped the muscles of her stomach

nerves fluttered in the pit of her stomach

nerves rippled low down in her stomach as she spoke the words

she asked, her stomach giving a curious twist as she said the words

she could feel a swirl of nervous knots in her stomach

she felt a (hollow feeling/weakness) in the pit of her stomach

she felt a fluttering of nerves in the pit of her stomach

she felt a knot of nerves in the pit of her stomach

she felt her stomach sink

she murmured, her stomach churning at the thought

she pressed a hand to her stomach

she replied, a fluttery feeling in her stomach

she said, (patting/touching) her stomach

she said, with a hollow feeling at the pit of her stomach

USAGE EXAMPLES

"Is he really coming over this evening?" *Her stomach muscles fluttered.*

"I'm sorry," *he said, guilt blooming in his stomach.* "I can't lie to you any longer."

She felt her stomach sink. "When did you find out?"

Body: Throat

a bubble of laughter rose in her throat (and escaped)

all the rest of the words stuck in her throat

a lump came into her throat

a lump seemed to rise in her throat as she spoke the words

a nerve quickened in her throat

a pulse (hammered/jarred/quickened) in her throat

a sigh caught in her throat

a sob arose in her throat

a sob caught in her throat

a stammer leapt nervously to her throat

a sudden unspeakable pain gripped her by the throat

a wedge of anger mixed with tears filled her throat

he gave a brief laugh, which he seemed to hold in his throat

he laughed low down in his throat

he laughed low in his throat

her breath caught (sharply) in her throat

her throat contracted with emotion

her throat had suddenly gone dry

her throat muscles tightened

her throat pulsed

her throat suddenly ached

her throat tightened (with tears)

her throat was parched

her throat was so dry that it hurt to speak

her throat went dry

her voice scraped her throat

he said, speaking deep in his throat

he was laughing deep in his throat

she asked, a frightened catch in her throat

she buried her face against his warm throat

she clasped her throat with her hand

she croaked, her throat parched

she felt a cry rising to her throat

she felt a curious constriction in her throat

she felt a fluttering in her throat and put her hand to it

she felt a lump at the back of her throat

she felt a lump come into her throat

she felt a lump in her throat

she felt a nervous tightening in her throat

she felt a pulse flutter in her throat

she felt as if her heart had come into her throat

she felt the breath catch in her throat

she laughed against his throat

she managed to suppress the tears swelling in her throat

she muttered, her dry throat rasping

she nodded, her throat was too dry for speech

she nodded, the breath knocked out of her throat

she put a hand to her throat

she said, feeling a sob rising in her throat

she said, her throat contracting painfully

she said, swallowing the lump forming in her throat

she said, swallowing the lump in her throat

she swallowed as if to ease the lump in her throat

she swallowed a sudden dryness from her throat

she swallowed the dryness from her throat

she swallowed the lump in her throat

she swallowed the lump of (emotion) in her throat

she swallowed the lump that came into her throat

she swallowed the nausea in her throat

she swallowed the nervous dryness from her throat

she whispered, a sob strangled in her throat

she whispered, her throat thick with (emotion)

shyness gripped her throat at the thought of (...)

something between a laugh and a sob escaped from her throat

something quivered in her throat and caught at her upper lip

tears rose up in her throat but she managed to quell them

the breath caught in her throat

the words caught (breathlessly) in her throat

the words half-died in her throat

the words jolted nervously from her throat

the words scraped her throat

the words seemed to catch in her throat

the words seemed to drag themselves from his throat

the words seemed to purr (from/in) his throat

the word tore from her throat

USAGE EXAMPLES

"Why can't you be happy for me?" *A lump came into her throat.*

"Do you really believe in magic?" *He laughed low in his throat.*

"I don't care what you think!" *she said, feeling a sob rising in her throat.*

Eyes

a flash of temper lighted her eyes

a flicker of irritation and impatience shone in his eyes

a glimmer of laughter came into her eyes

a sardonic smile gleamed in his eyes

amusement glinted in his eyes

as he spoke, his eyes stayed fixed on (...)

(emotion) flickered in his eyes

he asked her, a whimsical look in his eyes

he closed his eyes and tried to think

he gazed down into her eyes

he met her eyes moodily

he narrowed his eyes

he queried, his blue eyes twinkling

he raised his eyes and smiled at her

he raked his eyes over her (adjective) face

her blue eyes blazed into his

he replied slowly, his eyes evading hers

her eyes blazed with (emotion)

her eyes brightened

her eyes brightened at the words

her eyes darkened with pain

her eyes flashed to meet his

her eyes had lit up

her eyes held a flash of shock

her eyes held a puzzled look

her eyes lifted to meet his

her eyes lit up with indignation

her eyes misted with tears

her eyes softened a little

her eyes wavered from his

her eyes were fixed upon him

her eyes were glittering

he rubbed his eyes sleepily

he said, a meaningful look in his eyes

he said, closing his eyes in (emotion)

he said, his eyes fixed on the ground

he said, narrowing his eyes

he said as he stared into her eyes

he shot back, his eyes glittering with anger

he slid his eyes up and down her (adjective) body

he swept his eyes up and down her body

his dark eyes settled directly on hers

his eyes blazed down at her

his eyes dwelt on her lips as she spoke

his eyes flashed ominously

his eyes flicked over her

his eyes focused intently on her face

his eyes glinted

his eyes held her captive

his eyes held hers

his eyes looked stern

his eyes mocked her

his eyes narrowed as he searched her face

his eyes narrowed at the words

his eyes narrowed thoughtfully

his eyes raked hers

his eyes sank, and involuntarily he sighed

his eyes shifted nervously

his eyes shone angrily now

his eyes swept her up and down

his eyes watched her

his eyes were bleak as he looked at her

his eyes were hard and scornful

his eyes were suddenly as cold as ice

hot tears welled into her eyes

said (character), opening her eyes wide

she blushed and her eyes were downcast for a moment

she choked, her eyes (burning/filling) with tears

she could feel his eyes boring through her back

she could feel his eyes probing into her

she couldn't take her eyes away from him

she couldn't take her eyes from his face

she cried, protest in her eyes

she gazed at him with reproving eyes

she glanced up enquiringly into his (adjective) eyes

she looked at him with a desperate appeal in her eyes

she looked him straight in the eyes

she looked up at him with slight surprise in her eyes

she met his eyes

she murmured, her eyes downcast

she raised her eyes and looked at him (adverb)

she raised her eyes to his face

she responded, turning her eyes to the (noun)

she rolled her eyes at him

she said, blinking back tears

she said, dropping her eyes

she said, evading his eyes

she said, her eyes burning with (emotion)

she said, her eyes sparkling with laughter

she said, her eyes suddenly moist (with tears)

she said, trying her best to avoid his eyes

she said with tears in her eyes

she studied him with bright, curious eyes

she was transfixed by his eyes

she went on softly, her eyes on his

she whispered, her eyes wide with fright

she widened her eyes at him

something flashed in his eyes

tears gleamed in her eyes

there was horror in her eyes

triumph gleamed in his eyes

USAGE EXAMPLES

"You're naughty!" *A glimmer of laughter came into her eyes.*

"What did you say he did for a living?" *He narrowed his eyes.*

"You can't treat me like this," *she cried, protest in her eyes.*

Face

a look of (emotion) flashed over his face

a look of scorn flashed across his face

a mask of reserve seemed to cover her face

a smile creased his face

a smile lit up her face

a smile was spreading over her face

a sudden look of (emotion) passed across the (adjective) face

a teasing smile crossed his face

he agreed, his face like iron

he broke off and a frown clouded his face

he cradled her face in his hands

he flashed a smile at her anxious face

he framed her face with his hands (and looked deeply into her eyes)

he half-turned to face her

he pulled a mocking face at her

he pushed a hand over his face

he remarked, not a vestige of humor showing on his face

he responded, and she could feel his eyes searching her face

her face crinkled in (concern/confusion)

her face grew warm with shame

her face had gone as white as the wall behind her

her face was ashen

her face wrinkled in contempt

he said, cupping her face with both hands

he said, his face looking hard and shadowed

he said with a somber expression on his face

he sat looking at her, his face unreadable

he studied her face for a long moment, then he said

he swung to face her

he turned deliberately to face her

his eyes narrowed as he searched her face

his face (suddenly) became red with shame

his face became livid with anger

his face (darkened/hardened)

his face had a distant look

his face was dark and impassive

his face was grim (with anger)

his face was hard

his face wore a sudden formidable look

his formerly calm face was disturbed by a hard tightening of his jaw

she broke into tears and buried her face in her hands

she broke off as a frown darkened his face

she buried her face against his warm throat

she buried her face in her hands

she could feel her face blushing

she drew her face away from him

she exclaimed, her face flushing bright red

she made a face

she murmured, wiping the tears from her face

she pressed her face against him

she replied with a mutinous look on her face

she said, a shadow of dismay crossing her face

she said, her face bemused

she said, her face blushing in embarrassment

she said, her face crinkling in annoyance

she said, her face showing signs of (agitation/exhaustion/weariness)

she said with her face wrinkled in disgust

she saw a slight smile flicker across his face

she scanned his face

she spoke bravely, though the color had left her face

she stared at her own face in the mirror

she stared at the burnt-gold of his face

she studied his face in the dim light

she touched his face and slowly traced her fingers over his features

she turned her face quickly away

she turned suddenly to face him

she whispered, her face pale at the thought

the color had receded from her face

then his face became stern

USAGE EXAMPLES

"The things people say, eh?" *A smile creased his face.*

"I don't like your attitude," *he remarked, not a vestige of humor showing on his face.*

"Why are you still here?" *Her face wrinkled in contempt.*

Face: Cheeks

a dash of wild color entered her cheeks

a faint flush tinged her cheeks

a flush stole into her cheeks

a flush stung her cheeks

all the color receded from her cheeks

a pink flush came and went in her cheeks

a smile creased his lean cheek

a tear splashed to her cheek

a tear stole down her cheek

a wild pink color washed into her cheeks

color ebbed into her cheeks

color flamed into her cheeks

color had run back into her cheeks

color rushed into his cheeks

color stained her cheeks

color stormed into his cheeks

color stung her cheeks

grin lines slashed his cheeks

he ran a finger down her cheek

her cheeks burned

her cheeks burned as his eyes swept over her

her cheeks burned red with embarrassment

her cheeks crimsoned as she (...)

her cheeks flamed

her cheeks grew faintly pink

her cheeks grew hot at the thought of (...)

her cheeks grew pink as she (...)

her cheeks had taken on the hue of wild cherries

he stroked her cheek

his lips brushed her pink cheek

his warm fingers stroked her cheek

she brushed a teardrop from her cheek

she felt a tinge of heat (in/touch) her cheeks

she felt her cheeks grow warm

she felt her cheeks reddening

she felt the color steal into her cheeks

she gave his cheek a playful pinch

she murmured, a warmth in her cheeks

she reached out and stroked his cheek

she replied, a flush rising into her cheeks

she said, a coral flush tingling the tips of her cheekbones

she said, a flame on each cheekbone

she said, heat in her cheeks

she said, the color flowing into her cheeks

she saw a crease of amusement in his lean cheek

she touched his warm cheek

she wiped the tears from her cheeks (with the back of her hand)

the color deepened in her cheeks

the color had fled from her cheeks

the color returned to her cheeks

the flush deepened in her cheeks

USAGE EXAMPLES

All the color receded from her cheeks. "What do you mean?"

"Please forgive me, Simon." *A tear splashed to her cheek.*

"How dare you!" *Her cheeks grew faintly pink.*

Face: Eyebrows / Brows

a quizzical brow arched above his left eye

a thoughtful frown joined his eyebrows together

he arched a black brow

he arched an eyebrow in sardonic inquiry

he drew his eyebrows together in a frown

he quirked a black eyebrow

he quirked a dark eyebrow at her

he raised an eyebrow in amusement

he raised an eyebrow questioningly

her brow creased

her brows knitted together

her brows pulled together in a frown

he said, a thoughtful frown drawing his eyebrows together

he scrunched up his eyebrows thoughtfully

he slowly raised an eyebrow

he tilted an eyebrow

his brows drew together

his brows had merged into a savage line

his brows lifted in surprise

his brows were knitted in a thoughtful frown

his dark eyebrows drew together in a scowl

his eyebrows came together in a thoughtful frown

his eyebrows shot up

his heavy brows came together

his left eyebrow took a quizzical dip

she arched her eyebrows

she said, a line of worry materializing between her eyebrows

she said, her dark brows tangling in a scowl

she slowly arched an eyebrow

she wrinkled her brow

surprise lifted his black brows

USAGE EXAMPLES

"Really?" He quirked a black eyebrow.

Her brow creased. "What is she talking about?"

"Don't test me, boy!" she said, her dark brows tangling in a scowl.

Hair

he broke off and buried his face in her hair

he brushed a strand of hair back from his frowning forehead

he buried his lips in her hair

he drew his hands down her soft hair

he laughed against her hair

he pushed his fingers through her hair

he pushed his long fingers through her hair

he rumpled his black hair with a large hand

he said, a strand of black hair astray on his brow

he said, brushing a hand over his hair

he said, fingering her hair and discovering its texture

he said, his breath against her hair

he said, ruffling her hair playfully

he swept the chaotic hair from his eyes

he thrust a hand through his black hair

he thrust an impatient hand through his hair

he thrust the tumbling hair back from his eyes

he touched the wave of hair above her eyes

his breath stirred her hair

his eyes roamed over her hair and face

she brushed the soft wave of hair out of her eyes

she combed her fingers through her hair

she flung back her hair with a toss of her head

she flung the hair back from her brow

she flushed as she lifted a hand to her (adjective) hair

she glowered back at him through her tangled hair

she jerked the hair out of her eyes

she murmured, her dark hair spread across her pillow

she played with the wispy tendrils of her hair

she pushed a hand through her hair

she pushed distractedly at her hair

she pushed the (adjective) hair back from her eyes

she ran her fingers through her hair

she said, flicking her hair out of her eyes

she said, sliding a hand over his hair

she said, tossing her hair with a turn of the head

she said, toweling her hair

she smiled as she caressed his hair

she stroked the hair from his closed eyes

she swept the tousled hair back off her brow

she tossed her hair with disdain

she touched her hair

she twirled her hair with her fingers

she was glad that her hair veiled her expression

USAGE EXAMPLES

"I'll never let anything bad happen to you." *He pushed his fingers through her hair.*

"Okay," *he said, brushing a hand over his hair*, "back to the drawing board."

"This heat is killing me," *she said, flicking her hair out of her eyes.*

Head / Forehead

a frown creased her forehead

a sudden deep frown creased the man's forehead

a vein throbbed on his forehead

he didn't dare turn his head to face her

he dropped a quick kiss on her forehead

he inclined his dark head

he inclined his head gravely

he nodded his head

he paused and turned his head

he pressed his lips to her forehead

he raised his head

her forehead was beaded with moisture

her forehead was puckered in thought

her head was spinning, she could hardly think straight

he said, drooping his head

he said, pressing a hand to her forehead

he said with a brief tilt of his head

he said with shake of his head

he touched a hand to his forehead

he turned his head and stared at her

he wiped his forehead with the edge of his hand

his head lifted and met her gaze

she (pressed/put) a hand to her forehead

she asked, her forehead beading with sweat

she bent her head and looked mutinous

she bowed her head (slightly)

she broke off and her head seemed to swim

she drew a hand across her forehead

she fiercely shook her head

she flung back her head in laughter

she held her head high

she kissed his forehead

she murmured, her head slightly bowed

she pressed her fingers to her forehead

she said, a worried frown creasing her forehead

she said, ducking her head

she said, lowering her forehead

she said, resting her forehead against him

she shook a bewildered head

she shook her head

she shook her head (dumbly/mutely/tiredly/wildly)

she shook her head and avoided his glance

she shook her head at him

she shook her head firmly at him

she shook her head in disbelief

she slowly turned her head

she spoke with her head bowed

she started to shake her head, and then hesitated

she tilted her head and met his eyes

she tilted her head forward

she tossed back her head

she tossed her head

she twisted her head away

USAGE EXAMPLES

A frown creased her forehead. "This can't be right, can it?"

"I hate it here!" *he said, drooping his head.*

She fiercely shook her head. "No, I refuse!"

Mouth

an uncontrollable smile shook her mouth

a slow grin quirked his mouth

a smile crinkled her mouth

a smile curled on his mouth

a smile curled the edge of his mouth

a smile edged his mouth

a smile flickered at the edge of his mouth

a smile pulled his mouth to one side

a smile quivered on her mouth

a smile shaped the woman's mouth

a smile touched his mouth

a smile tugged at the corner of his mouth

a smirk sprang to his mouth

a wry little smile quirked his mouth

he asked, a smile at the edge of his mouth

he forced his mouth into a smile

he murmured against her mouth

her mouth tensed

her mouth twisted into a knowing smile

her mouth was tightly pursed

her mouth went dry

he said, a corner of his mouth quirking with amusement

he said, a grin of amusement on his mouth

he said, a hint of mockery edging his mouth

he said, a smile thinning his mouth

he said, a teasing quirk at the corner of his mouth

he said, his mouth faintly mocking

he said, one side of his mouth twisting into a smile

his mouth compressed into a hard line

his mouth gave a sardonic twist

his mouth gave a slight twist

his mouth grew mocking

his mouth hardened

his mouth jerked into a grin

his mouth moved in a smile

his mouth pulled to one side in a grimace

his mouth thinned

his mouth twisted

his mouth was cynical

one corner of his mouth twitched slightly

she breathed against his mouth

she looked at his mouth

she noticed the lines beside his mouth deepen

she pouted her mouth at him

she replied, feeling her mouth go dry

she said, her heart in her mouth

she said, her mouth crinkling into a smile

she said through a mouthful of (...)

she said with a sensuous twist of her lips

she saw his mouth twist sarcastically

the ghost of a smile brushed her mouth

there was a twist to his mouth

the words leapt out of her mouth almost of their own accord

the words were out of her mouth before she could stop them

USAGE EXAMPLES

"She likes you." *A smile crinkled her mouth.*

"Did they see you?" *Her mouth went dry.*

There was a twist to his mouth. "Tomorrow will be different."

Mouth: Breathed

he breathed deeply

he broke off and took a deep breath

he drew a deep, audible breath

he drew a deep, harsh breath

he drew in his breath sharply

her breath caught on a sigh

her breath caught sharply in her throat

her breath quickened

he said, his warm breath fanning her skin

he said, slowly releasing his breath

he slowly released his breath

he took a deep breath

he whispered, his warm breath against her temple

his breath stirred against her neck

his breath stirred her hair

his warm breath fanned her skin

she barely breathed the word

she breathed

she breathed a quiet sigh of relief

she breathed the words

she caught her breath

she caught her breath, shocked

she caught her breath audibly

she drew a breathless sigh

she drew a shaky breath

she felt the breath catch in her throat

she gasped for breath

she gave a breathless laugh

she held her breath

she paused for breath

she said, catching her breath

she said, her breathing quickening

she said breathlessly

she spoke breathlessly

she took a deep, steadying breath

she took a deep breath of air

she waited breathlessly for his reply

she was breathing quickly now

the breath caught in her throat

USAGE EXAMPLES

"Is Helen alright?" *He drew a deep, audible breath.*

"Let's go out tonight," *he said, his warm breath fanning her skin.*

She was breathing quickly now. "Kiss me!"

Mouth: Laughed

a brief laugh broke from her

a laugh broke through her lips

he answered with a soft laugh

he gave a brief laugh

he gave a gruff laugh

he gave an exasperated laugh

he gave a shaken laugh

he gave a small derisive laugh

he laughed against her throat

he laughed as he spoke

he laughed at the very idea

he laughed lazily

he laughed low (down) in his throat

he laughed to himself (in satisfaction)

he laughingly murmured

he laughingly shook his head

her laughter rang out

he said, with a slight laugh

he said with an indulgent laugh

he said with a shrug and a laugh

he softly laughed

he was actually laughing as he said it

he was laughing at her

he was laughing deep in his throat

laughter came into her eyes

she broke into a short laugh

she broke into spontaneous laughter

she broke in with a laugh

she couldn't help but laugh

she forced a laugh

she gave a scoffing laugh

she gave a throaty little laugh

she had to laugh

she half laughed

she heard a little laugh escape him

she heard him laugh

she laughed

she laughed back

she laughed in confusion

she laughed shyly

she made herself laugh

she met his eyes and gave a nervous laugh

she said with a laugh

she was shaking with laughter

the woman laughed with delight

USAGE EXAMPLES

"You win," *he answered with a soft laugh.*

"Of course not!" *He laughingly shook his head.* "What do you take me for?"

"Is it always like this?" *She laughed shyly.*

Mouth: Lips

a (adjective) smile came and went on her lips

a (adjective) smile clung to his lips

a cynical smile twisted his lips

a sardonic smile flickered on his lips

a smile flickered on her lips

a smile played about his lips

a smile ran around his lips

a smile took possession of her lips

a smile tugged at her lips

a smile was on the edge of his lips

as soon as the words escaped from her lips, she wished she could take them back

as soon as the words escaped her lips she regretted them

a sudden sigh escaped from her lips

a thin smile edged his lips

a tremor of a smile (came to/touched) her lips

a vagrant smile touched her lips

he allowed his lips to quirk

he buried his lips in her hair

he pressed a napkin to his lips

he replied, a grin on his lips

her lips asked the question

her lips curled like flames

her lips fell apart

her lips formed an oval of surprise

her lips moved in a smile

her lips quivered

her lips trembled around the words

her lips trembled into a smile

her lips twisted with scorn

her lips were tense around the words

her lips were thin with rage

her lips were tremulous

her name broke from his lips

he said, a curl to his lips

he said, a mocking little smile playing (about/on) his lips

he said, a wry smile touching his lips

he said, his eyes fixed upon her lips

he said, slipping a (...) between his lips

he said, smoke curling from his lips

his eyes dwelt on her lips

his fingers came to her lips as she spoke

his lips brushed across her forehead

his lips brushed her cheek

his lips curled

his lips curled (slowly) into a smile

his lips curled around the words

his lips curled in self-appreciative amusement

his lips expressed amusement

his lips moved in a momentary smile

his lips quirked

his lips twisted when she said that

his lips twitched

his lips were drawn into a thin line

his lips were edged by a faintly mocking smile

his lips were quirking as his gaze drifted to her (...)

his voice brought a reluctant smile to her lips

she (dampened/eased/licked/moistened/wet) her dry lips with the tip of her tongue

she bit her lip

she felt his lips against her (forehead/lashes/temple)

she felt his lips touch her hair

she forced a smile to her lips

she huffed, her lips sewn into a grimace

she laid a hand to his lips

she moistened her lips

she pouted her lips at him

she raised her glass to her lips

she said, (blotting/dabbing) her lips with (...)

she said, and a tremor shook her lips

she said, a wry smile lifting the corners of her lips

she said, her lips tremulous

she said, laughter breaking through her lips

she said, pursing her lips

she said, turning away from the smile on his lips

she said with a little twist to her lips

she shaped her lips into a smile

she spoke through pursed lips

smoke curled from his lips (as he spoke)

smoke drifted (lazily) from his lips

the question came from the lips of (...)

the retort sprang to her lips of its own accord

the words faded on her lips when she (...)

the words leapt to her lips

the words left her lips before she could stop them

USAGE EXAMPLES

A thin smile edged his lips. "Are we having fun yet?"

She moistened her lips. "Is this really necessary, Donald?"

"I see you don't agree." *She spoke through pursed lips.*

Mouth: Smile

for a moment longer he smiled

he (adverb) smiled

he nodded and slowly smiled

her eyes flashed, and then she smiled

her smile faded

he said, and they smiled at one another

he shot a grin at her

he smiled (adverb) to himself

he smiled, almost to himself

he smiled, and a hint of arrogance glimmered in his eyes

he smiled, as if reading her thoughts

he smiled, but his eyes were empty

he smiled, taking in (...)

he smiled, uncaring that she (...)

he smiled, unsurprised that (...)

he smiled a brief sardonic smile

he smiled a little

he smiled as he said it

he smiled as if he enjoyed the thought of (...)

he smiled at her

he smiled at her exclamation of delight

he smiled at her flight of fancy

he smiled at her insistence

he smiled at the thought

he smiled at the way (she/her) (...)

he smiled back

he smiled down at her (with brief amusement)

he smiled down at her, his teeth glimmering against his dark skin

he smiled down deliberately into her eyes

he smiled grimly as (...)

he smiled in his grave way

he smiled into her (eyes/face)

he smiled rather dangerously

he smiled through his cigarette smoke

he smiled through narrowed eyes

he smiled up at her impudently

he smiled wistfully upon her

he smiled with a touch of mockery

he smiled with his lips, but his eyes (remained/revealed) (...)

he smiled with satisfaction

his eyes closed, and he smiled to himself

his lips smiled faintly

his lips smiled slowly in self-appreciative amusement

she braved his eyes and smiled (adverb)

she forced a (demure) smile

she grimaced as she smiled

she half smiled (at the thought)

she slowly shook her head and smiled

she smiled (adverb)

she smiled, and then sighed

she smiled, but deep inside she (...)

she smiled, but it ached a little on her mouth

she smiled, but she was thinking to herself that (...)

she smiled, grateful for (...)

she smiled, recalling that (...)

she smiled, revealing a dimple in her (left/right) cheek

she smiled, though she still felt as if (...)

she smiled across the table at (character)

she smiled a little as she thought of (...)

she smiled a little at his (...)

she smiled a little to herself as (...)

she smiled an agreement

she smiled and breathed again

she smiled and for the first time in a long time

she smiled and nodded

she smiled as if fine

she smiled as she recalled the (...)

she smiled as she spoke

she smiled at him in a slightly absent way

she smiled at him with doubt in her eyes

she smiled at that

she smiled at the idea

she smiled at thoughts of (...)

she smiled back at him

she smiled back at him rather tensely

she smiled but didn't look at him

she smiled but felt at the same time a (...)

she smiled faintly at the thought

she smiled her relief

she smiled her secret smile

she smiled in answer

she smiled in memory

she smiled most flirtatiously at him

she smiled rather wistfully

she smiled reassuringly at him

she smiled sweetly as she said it

she smiled to herself

she smiled up at him

she smiled with a certain wistfulness

she smiled with a touch of disdain

she smiled with delight

she smiled with eagerness

she smiled with the utmost satisfaction

she smiled wryly to herself and wondered

she then smiled (adverb) at him

suddenly the man smiled

the girl smiled happily

then he shrugged and smiled (adverb)

the woman actually smiled

the woman smiled maliciously

understanding dawned in her eyes and she smiled

USAGE EXAMPLES

"I don't blame you for wanting it." *He smiled, as if reading her thoughts.*

"Anything else I can help you with?" *He smiled with satisfaction.*

"It's alright, dear." *She smiled reassuringly at him.*

Mouth: Teeth

he bared his teeth

he bit the words out with his strong white teeth

he drew in air between his teeth

he fixed his eyes on her face, his teeth gritted

he grinned, his teeth flashing white against his tanned face

her teeth bit down on her lip

her teeth caught at her lip

he said, displayed his perfect teeth

he said, his teeth glinting in a friendly smile

he said, his teeth glinting white as he gazed down at her

he said through his teeth

he smiled, showing his bone-white teeth

his smile showed a neat line of white teeth

his smile was a flash of white teeth

his teeth clenched angrily around the words

his teeth flashed in a smile

his teeth gleamed in a half smile

his teeth gleamed white against his dark skin

his teeth glimmered

his teeth glimmered in a smile

his teeth glinted in a brief smile

his teeth seemed to bite out the words

his teeth snapped in a laugh

his teeth snapped in spite

his teeth were a flash of white against his bronzed skin

his white teeth flashed in a smile

she caught her bottom lip between her teeth

she clenched her teeth in a grimace

she drew her lower lip between her teeth

she pleaded through chattering teeth

she said, showing her white teeth in a smile

she said, sinking her teeth into her lower lip

she said it through her teeth

she said through clenched teeth

she spoke through gritted teeth

the edge of his teeth showed in a brief smile

USAGE EXAMPLES

"I was hoping you were available for dinner." *Her teeth bit down on her lip*.

"What time do you want me to pick you up?" *His teeth flashed in a smile*.

"Get out," *she said through clenched teeth*.

Mouth: Voice

anger and nerves shook her voice

a sudden note of contempt crept into his voice

a voice hissed

a voice murmured

came (character)'s soothing voice

he asked, in a voice devoid of emotion

he asked in a dangerous voice

he demanded, his voice almost savage

he interrupted in a loud voice

her delight rang warm in her voice

her voice cracked

her voice faded

her voice held a tremor

her voice shook just a little, betraying her true feelings

her voice shook slightly

her voice shook with fury

her voice throbbed

her voice was laden with emotion

her voice was quiet and tense

her voice was so husky as to be almost inaudible

he said, a hint of mockery in his voice

he said, a note of firmness in his voice

he said, astoundment in his voice

he said, his voice emptied of emotion

he said, his voice firm as a rock

he said, his voice suddenly empty

he said, in a deliberate voice

he said in a deep voice that seemed to vibrate along her nerves

he said in a dry tone of voice

he said in the most curious tone of voice

he said with his menacing tone of voice

he spoke in a consoling voice

he spoke in an amused voice

he spoke in a rather weary tone of voice

he spoke the words in a low, pained voice

his tone of voice was sardonic

his voice came from a distance

his voice came low from his throat

his voice cut across her thoughts

his voice cut like a whip across her thoughts

his voice grew caustic

his voice had a savage edge to it

his voice had risen almost to a scream

his voice had softened a little

his voice held a bitter note

his voice held a distant note

his voice lashed at her

his voice matched the hardness of his gaze

his voice mocked her

his voice softened

his voice was harsh

his voice was laced with concern

his voice was low-pitched, almost crooning

his voice was suddenly as hard as steel

his voice went rough

his voice went soft and almost dangerous

sarcasm rang in his deep voice

she accused him in a frigid voice

she asked, her voice sounding strained all of a sudden

she asked, in a reluctant tone of voice

she asked in a cool, tempered voice

she asked in a low, shaky voice

she asked in a polite voice

she caught the sudden note of hardness in his voice

she fought to keep her voice steady

she heard the faint catch in his voice

she heard the smile in his voice

she kept her voice steady

she lowered her voice

she replied, her voice growing increasingly shaky

she said, a tinge of apprehension in her voice

she said, her voice husky but subdued

she said, her voice husky with tears

she said, in a cold voice

she said, in a rather strained voice

she said, keeping her voice low

she said, making her voice cool

she said in a choked voice

she said in a cool voice

she said in a low, fierce voice

she said in a thrilled voice

she spoke in a strained voice

she spoke in a strangled voice

she spoke in her most demure voice

she spoke the words in a barely audible voice

she stiffened at the curt note in his voice

she tried to keep her voice steady

snapped a woman's voice

something in his voice made her look up

the crisp voice cut in

the deep voice echoed

the panic pitched her voice almost to a scream

there was a deep note in his voice

there was an edge to his voice

there was an excited catch in her voice

there was ice in his voice

the sarcasm deepened in his voice

the voice broke in on her thoughts

the voice was harsh

when she finally spoke, her voice was hesitant

USAGE EXAMPLES

"What's your name?" *he asked in a dangerous voice.*

"Stay the hell away from him!" *Her voice shook with fury.*

"Susan can do whatever she wants." *His voice held a bitter note.*

Nose

a tear (fell/trickled) down the side of her nose

cigarette smoke slid from his (adjective) nose

(grinning/smiling), she tapped a finger against the tip of (character)'s (adjective) nose

he dropped a kiss (onto/on the tip of) her nose

he flared his nostrils

he lifted his nose and sniffed

he looked down his nose

he ran a finger across the bridge of his nose

her nose took a scornful tilt

he said, staring down his nose at her

he slid the (glasses/spectacles) off his nose

he touched his handkerchief to his (adjective) nose

his nostrils drew in the crisp air

remarked (character) with a scornful tilt of her nose

said (character), putting her nose in the air

said (character) as she powdered her nose

she (crinkled/scrunched) her nose (at him)

she buried her nose in her cup, trying to avoid his gaze

she drew (...) to her nose

she looked down the slope of her nose at (...)

she peered down her nose at him

she perched her (glasses/spectacles) (back) on her nose

she put her nose to the (...)

she rubbed a finger against her (adjective) nose

she rubbed her nose against his

she said (adverb), her nose tilting upward

she said, a haughty tilt to her nose

she said, dabbing at her nose with a handkerchief

she said, her nose in her drink

she said, pressing her nose to the window

she said, wrinkling her nose

she tilted her nose (in the air)

she tilted her nose in scorn

she took hold of (...) and held it up to her nose

she took out her compact and powdered her nose

she turned up her nose (at him)

she turned up her nose at the idea of (...)

she wriggled her nose above her glass of (...)

she wrinkled her nose (like a rabbit)

she wrinkled her nose as if she had smelled something bad

she wrinkled her nose at him in disgust

she wrinkled her nose with disapproval

the nostrils of his (adjective) nose were flaring

the smoke tickled her nose

USAGE EXAMPLES

He lifted his nose and sniffed. "Is that roast chicken I smell?"

"You can't do anything right, can you?" *he said, staring down his nose at her.*

"Leave us," *she said, a haughty tilt to her nose.*

Also by Dahlia Evans

Thinking Like A Romance Writer – The Sensual Writer's Sourcebook of Words and Phrases

"This invaluable resource is a must have for any aspiring romance writer!"

In the world of romance writing, one of the most important components in an author's repertoire is their use of descriptive words and phrases. This aspect of romance writing is so often neglected, usually with disastrous results; a novel that reads like a badly written script.

Fortunately, there's now a way for any writer, regardless of their experience, to get a huge head-start writing in this profitable genre. It's a secret resource that romance writers don't want you to know about!

Dahlia Evans has compiled a romance writing thesaurus unlike anything ever published. This reference book is filled to the brim with words and phrases gathered from hundreds of bestselling romance novels. Using this book you will be able to describe intimate encounters of every kind without breaking a sweat.

Inside You'll Discover:

* 8,500 words and phrases sorted into 37 categories.

* Thousands of words you can use to describe each part of the body.

* Words that describe each of the five senses; taste, touch, sight, sound, smell.

* Words to describe feelings and emotions.

* Words that describe facial expressions.

* Hundreds of words to describe intimacy.

Thinking Like A Romance Writer is the culmination of hundreds of hours of research and is a book destined to become a classic in the field of romance writing instruction.

Printed in Great Britain
by Amazon